5/04

if
you
want
to be a

WITCH

about edain mccoy

Edain McCoy became a self-initiated Witch in 1981 and underwent a formal initiation in 1983 with a large San Antonio coven. She has been researching alternative spiritualities since her teens, when she was first introduced to the kabballah. Since that time, she has studied a variety of magickal traditions, including Celtic, Appalachian, Curanderismo, Wiccan, Jewitchery, and Irish Wittan. *If You Want to Be a Witch* is her eighteenth book.

to write to the author

If you wish to contact the author or would like more information about this book, please write to the author in care of Llewellyn Worldwide and we will forward your request. Both the author and publisher appreciate hearing from you, but Llewellyn Worldwide cannot guarantee that every letter can be answered, but all will be forwarded. Please write to:

Edain McCoy
℅ Llewellyn Worldwide
P.O. Box 64383, Dept. 0-7387-514-4
St. Paul, MN 55164-0383, U.S.A.

Please enclose a self-addressed stamped envelope for reply, or one dollar to cover costs. If you are outside the U.S.A., please enclose an international postal reply coupon.

Many of Llewellyn's authors have websites with additional information and resources. For more information, please visit our Web site at www.llewellyn.com.

Edain McCoy

a practical introduction to the craft

if
you
want
to be a

WITCH

2004
Llewellyn
Publications
St. Paul, Minnesota
55164-0383, U.S.A.

First Edition
First Printing, 2004

Cover photo © 2003 by Brand X Pictures
Cover design by Gavin Dayton Duffy

All internal illustrations from Llewellyn Art Department

Library of Congress Cataloging-in-Publication Data
McCoy, Edain, 1957–
    If you want to be a witch: a practical introduction to the craft /
    Edain McCoy.—1st ed.
        p. cm.
    Includes bibliographical references and index.
    ISBN 0-7387-0514-4
    1. Witchcraft. I. Title.
    BF157.M455 2004
    133.4'3—dc22 2003065974

Llewellyn Worldwide does not participate in, endorse, or have any authority or responsibility concerning private business transactions between our authors and the public.
    All mail addressed to the author is forwarded but the publisher cannot, unless specifically instructed by the author, give out an address or phone number.
    Any Internet references contained in this work are current at publication time, but the publisher cannot guarantee that a specific location will continue to be maintained. Please refer to the publisher's Web site for links to authors' Web sites and other sources.

Llewellyn Publications
A Division of Llewellyn Worldwide, Ltd.
P.O. Box 64383, Dept. 0-7387-0514-4
St. Paul, MN 55164-0383, U.S.A.
www.llewellyn.com

Printed in the United States of America

Also by Edain McCoy

Witta
A Witch's Guide to Faery Folk
The Sabbats
How to Do Automatic Writing
Celtic Myth and Magick
Lady of the Night
Entering the Summerland
The Witch's Coven
Making Magick
Mountain Magick
Celtic Women's Spirituality
Astral Projection for Beginners
Bewitchments
Enchantments
Ostara
Spellworking for Covens
Advanced Witchcraft

Forthcoming

Karmic and Past Life Tarot

contents

so, you think you wanna be a witch?

Merry meet!

My name is Edain, and I've been a Witch for more than twenty years.

No, this isn't an introduction to a twelve-step program. "Merry Meet" is our traditional greeting to others who follow our ways—that is, others who follow earth and nature religions. It expresses our wishes for joyous and fruitful gatherings of those of us who worship in the fullness of nature, in what we sometimes refer to as the Old Religion. When we leave one another we say, "Merry part, and merry meet again." This is an expression of the good things we wish for others and our hope that our links in the web of existence will continue to flourish.

Were you reading closely? Did you catch the word "religion" attached to the practice of Witchcraft?

First, utmost, and beyond all other concerns, Witchcraft is a *religion*, probably one of the oldest on the planet, and one that gets new adherents daily all around the world. They may worship pantheons you're not familiar with, but they are trying to follow a positive path to the creators. Understanding this is not only your lesson number one, but a sentence you should emblazon upon your brain in flashing neon so it will never be forgotten:

Witchcraft is a religion, and its primary purpose is the worship of and the seeking of reunion with the being or beings who created all life.

It may not be easy at first for you to make that mental leap when many churches and society in general have for centuries hammered into people's brains the evils of Witchcraft. (Note that none of them can give you a valid explanation of those evils; they're just sure they're there.) On the other hand, when seeking solid information on the Craft suitable for the beginner at your local bookstore, the shelves seem to groan under the weight of all the books on Witchcraft and its related disciplines. It can overwhelm not only novices but intermediate students as well.

Where do you start?

You start right here, with this primer on basic Witchcraft. If you picked up this book, I assume you're interested in Witchcraft—"the Craft," as we say—or, at the very least, you're curious to learn more about this fast-growing and thriving faith. For the next two hundred pages or so, I'll be your guide into this spiritual movement that is both the oldest and newest on the planet. I'll try to help you sort out the confusing names and concepts that bombard you from the book stacks, and I'll try to steer you in the direction you want to go.

Don't worry if another newcomer picks out different books than you. We all have unique ways of learning, our own talents, and our own interests. Some authors will resonate with you, others may leave you unmoved. Glance through everything first, then select one or two books to start with. By the time you've worked through those, you'll know if this is the path you wish to travel in this lifetime.

in the beginning . . .

What do you already know about Witchcraft—or perhaps I should I ask, what do you *think* you already know? Why are you interested? There are easier ways to live your life than to be a part of any minority. What do you expect to get out of Witchcraft that makes the quest worth the struggle, and what do you expect to give back to it? Will you wear your religion with pride for all to see? Will you be an in-your-face militant, a sort of Witchy fundamentalist? Will you quietly walk your spiritual path alone with your deities or seek contacts for friendship, exchange of information, and perhaps group or coven worship?

What all Witches have in common is that we follow a nature- or earth-based religion. However, we each tread a slightly different path in our search for our creator, and each of our lives is filled with varying needs and desires, but, with faith and effort, we all hope to end up in the same place.

Before we begin, I want to prepare you for the flood of names and terms that accompanies the Craft. Witchcraft, sometimes referred to as Wicca or Eclectic Wicca, comprises the indigenous religions of western Europe, making it collectively one of the oldest religions on the planet. A Witch and a Wiccan may or may not be the same thing. Wicca began as a specific Anglo-Welsh tradition in England around the turn of the twentieth century, but today it is a tag often attached to other traditions (Celtic Wicca, Russian Wicca, etc.). There are two possible origins of the word "Witch," one being the Old English *wyk* meaning "to shape" or "to bend," and the other being the Anglo-Saxon *wit* meaning "to possess knowledge or wisdom." From "wyk" come the Craft words "wicce" and also the modern English word "wicked." From the Anglo-Saxon root word "wit," we get the Craft words "wita" and "witta." Like Wicca, the terms "Wicce" and "Witta" have ceased to be spiritual descriptions in their own right, and it's not uncommon to see "Wicce" or "Witta" combined with other cultural labels to create an entirely new Pagan tradition.

It may surprise you to know that both men and woman are called Witches. The term "warlock" is thought to be an old Scottish term meaning "oath breaker" or "sorcerer."

The word "warlock" is rarely, if ever, used as a label for a Pagan man. In fact, many men find it insulting.

Two thousand years ago, Europeans did not define themselves as Witches or Wiccans. Even the word "Pagan," derived from the Latin *paganus*, meaning "people of the earth," wasn't one people applied to themselves. The labeling of various cultural Craft traditions as Wicca, Wicce, Wita, Witta, or Wice is a twentieth-century addition to the Craft. In the clan and tribal societies of old Europe, religion and spirituality were woven into the fabric of everyday life. One might be said to possess *wicca* or have *witta*, meaning that he possessed a special skill or knowledge, but such a person would not label his religion that way. He would have been more likely to say he was a follower of a particular patron deity or was a priest of a deity within a specific cultural pantheon.

For the purposes of this book, I will be using the terms "Witchcraft" and "Wicca" to refer to western European, earth-based religions and those that came to North America with European immigrants. The word "Pagan" will be used to denote the follower of any earth- or nature-based spiritual system or religion. In other words, all Wiccans and Witches are Pagans, but not all Pagans are Witches or Wiccans.

Another word you might hear applied to a broad groups of Pagans is "Heathen." Many Germanic traditions prefer this appellation instead of "Pagan." The word simply means "of the heath" or "of the country."

There are now hundreds of cultural traditions that have been revived, pieced together, and compiled by modern Pagans (sometimes called neo-Pagans). At some point, you will be exposed to many of them. They each have variations in their practices and beliefs, but they are all valid expressions of an ancient spirituality in the modern world. As long as the practitioners are harming no one, they deserve your respect and, in turn, they should give your spiritual path the same consideration.

what next?

Traditionally, it takes a year and a day of study before you can undergo an initiation and be called a Witch or Wiccan rather than a dedicant, apprentice, or student. At that time, you may do a self-initiation or be initiated by a coven or another Witch. If you display the proper knowledge one expects of someone who's put in a serious year and a day of work, no one will question your right to call yourself a Witch. However, if you come across followers of a specific tradition (such as Gardnerian, Alexandrian, British Traditional, Seax-Wica, Stegheria, Dianic, Faerie, etc.) and you wish to be part of that tradition, you will have to learn its unique practices and be initiated into that sect. This extended study time is common in traditions ruled under a strict hierarchy (dedicant, first degree, initiate, second degree, priest/ess, high priest or priestess, third degree, elder, etc.). You will need to study with someone from within that tradition, learn its special rituals and tradition secrets, and then be initiated if you wish to be called a Witch of that tradition.

Many Witches, especially those who do not have or want ties to a coven or other group, tend to shun traditional labels. Instead, they will take their cultural heritage or their family's seasonal customs, and create their own private ways of ritual and worship. This is called solitary practice.

Eclectic Wicca, the most common type of Witchcraft practiced in North America, draws from the practices of many cultures and remains open to anyone who is interested in learning and working within its generous parameters. Many eclectic Craft study circles are operating around the major cities of the United States, the United Kingdom, and Canada. Look in alternative newspapers, and on bulletin boards at health food stores, and always ask in an occult shop. Many times the shop will act as a go-between to help people link up with others who share a similar vision.

starting your own book of shadows

Before you begin to learn any more about Witchcraft, before you rush out to the occult shop, I encourage you to start compiling a Book of Shadows in a simple loose-leaf notebook. Witchcraft has no single holy book as many other religions do. Each coven or group of Witches who work together will have its own Book of Shadows, and each individual Witch within the coven and each solitary Witch will have her own book.

As you read through this book, you should start recording in your Book of Shadows your impressions, your dreams, what you like and don't like, and what you want and don't want. You can change your mind later about any aspect of the Craft, and you will—probably more than once—but for now this is your starting point.

After you're done with this book, your Book of Shadows will be your most useful and personal magick and ritual tool during your first years as a Witch. In it, you will record your thoughts, your spells, your potion recipes, festival recipes, ritual texts, dreams, divination results, and just about anything else you can think of as your integrate Witchcraft into every aspect of your life. If you later join a coven or have one or more teachers, they may give you parts of their books to copy into yours. Or you may end up with two books, one for your personal use and another for use within your coven.

Your book doesn't have to be fancy, but if fancy appeals to you, there are beautiful journals and other attractive blank books available. I started out using them myself but found a loose-leaf notebook held more information, and it allowed me to reorganize pages as needed.

No one knows for sure how old this practice of keeping a Book of Shadows is, but it could be that it was borrowed from ceremonial magick or other forms of wizardry that were practiced by the literate and educated upper classes during the Middle Ages. They called their spell books *grimoires*, a word of uncertain etymology, but which is possibly an Old French term to describe the changing of one substance to another. Another theory is that it comes from an Old Norman English word that may have been the origin of the modern English words "grammar" and "glamour."

The name "Book of Shadows" comes from the concept that rituals and spells dwell in thoughtforms only, hiding in the shadows of our minds, rituals not fully formed until enacted by the Witch. Another theory states that, during the Witchhunting hysteria, Witches met in the dark, skulking through shadows of the moon to their meeting places. The thoughtforms origin makes more sense because, again, we're dealing with the lives and folk beliefs of poor and illiterate people.

Write it out

To get the most out of your book you must *write it yourself*. Words written by you stick in your head more securely than words that are spoken by you or read to you. Writing is a slow process, and by writing things down, you'll find that concepts will clarify themselves and new questions will arise to guide your spiritual growth. If you're not going to get the most out of writing, then you'd better rethink your interest in Witchcraft because most of it is just plain old hard work and requires a substantial investment of time and personal energy to master.

Many modern Witches keep their Books of Shadows on computers, and this is fine as long as the Witch types the information himself. All this means is that photocopying and downloading information are not the ways to keep your book. Do your own typing or writing to get the most benefit from it.

challenging your mind

I picked up my first book on Witchcraft in 1972, but it was almost another full decade before I knew I wanted to dedicate myself to serious study. At that time covens, teachers, and reliable books were scarce. Today, Wicca and other forms of Paganism are among the fastest growing spiritual movements in the world. Books, covens, teachers, and other students are everywhere and Witches are present in every level of society.

Whether you teach yourself, work with other beginners, have a study group with access to a teacher or teachers, or have a whole teaching coven to help you, you will be challenged by the powers of the universe and by your God and Goddess as you progress toward the end of your year and a day. You will be expected to do much reading—not just of Craft books, but of astronomy, astrology, mythology, physics, and botany. You will learn to expand your thinking to include multiple realities, omnipresent time, and the fact that many paths and ideas can lead us to reunion with our creator or creators, which is the ultimate purpose of any religion.

You will run into lots of other Pagans along the way, some of whom you will like and others you won't. This is because we're not our religion; we're just people, and that means we're not perfect. This is also the reason some covens hum with high energy and other just lie around doing nothing. Some Witches who've been through these immature rumbles often leave for another coven or for solitary practice. If you pick up Pagan magazines, you will often hear all this nonspiritual teeth-gnashing called a Witch War or, my favorite, Witchcrap. Unfortunately, no religion has found a way to keep its zealots under control. Those who practice with us but naysay every point create a chasm within good covens by turning their focuses on infighting and pointless arguments.

the student witch

A good Witch will always remember that, for the rest of his life, long after that first year and a day is complete, he will still be a student. We are all always students and all always teachers. Even after more than twenty years in the Craft, I learn new things all the time, often from newcomers. This is another illustration of the wheel of existence on which we ride through time and space. Nothing is linear, everything is a circular, coming to us, going from us, and returning to us again.

As you study Witchcraft, read with a critical eye for things you like and things you don't like and for things that don't strike you as accurate. This should be done whenever you read a Craft book or when discussing a book's merits with others. I've made many mistakes by accepting things I was told early on without using my powers of reasoning. Blind faith is disastrous in a religion called the Craft of the Wise. I've found blatant mistakes in many Craft books, even my own. Live and learn.

To be the best Witch you can be, resolve to purge your mind of any and all images Hollywood has shown you, then hop on your inner broomstick and ride with me into the world of the moon, the sun, and magickal living. Only by experiencing knowledge can it become wisdom and be of any use to us spiritually. Witchcraft is a lifelong commitment—not just to a religion but to a way of living in harmony with all other beings. The learning and teaching process is another one of our cycles that never ends. How high you fly is up to you. Discover your needs, test your personal powers, seek out your patron deities, and dig in the dirt that is the Great Mother who gave you life, for only then will you know for sure *if you want to be a Witch.*

the birth and rebirth of witchcraft

Interest in Witchcraft has exploded throughout the last half of the twentieth century. However, the roots of Witchcraft reach far back into prehistory, and it's important for a new Witch to understand something of the tortuous past of her chosen spiritual path. A Witch has to know where she's been to know where she is, and she has to know where she is to know how to get where she's going.

everything old is new again

Witchcraft maintains an unusual position among the world's religions in that it is both the oldest and the newest. The Craft can also be counted among the religions in which one is born again . . . uh . . . and again, and again, and again, and again.

The earliest religious impulses of humanity were centered on the daily activities of one's tribe or clan. They gave honor to the forces of nature, which could bless or kill without warning, and they likely used blood sacrifices and other magickal thinking to propitiate the deities and garner their favor. Cave drawings from Europe show shamanistic activities that appear to be designed to ensure a fruitful hunt and abundance throughout the dreaded European winters.

These early humans lived close to nature, developing a keen sense of what present events were omens of future events. The moon was their first calendar, and ancient peoples viewed the cycles of the sun as manifestations of a divine force governing their lives. The three phases of the moon represented the Triple Goddess—virgin, mother, and crone—and the sun was the embodiment of the God who was her son, lover, and consort.

The remnants of early tribal or clan religions are still practiced today in what we refer to as "famtrads," a shortening of the term "family tradition." Many modern Witches report unusual rites, unique to their families, even when their families are ostensibly Christian or Jewish. These are part of the oral customs of the old clan religions that have been passed down as family traditions even though a skilled eye can see the Pagan influence behind them. Today there are many of these families who draw a large portion of their spiritual practices from customs passed down from one generation to another. Witches in these famtrads are sometimes referred to as "hereditary" Witches or as practitioners of hereditary Witchcraft.

Early humanity was nomadic, moving their villages with the herds and the cycle of the seasons. This gave rise to the attachment of deities to specific places, objects, or animals. These deities of rivers, stones, animals, etc. are still honored in the Craft today as both divine manifestations of nature and as the elemental or nature spirits we refer to as faeries.

With the rise of farming and herding cultures, villages became rooted to specific places. Humanity saw the rise of a special class of men and women who displayed specific skills in controlling or predicting the forces of nature. These individuals—the first priests—became the tribes' intermediaries between the divine and humanity. This freed others for the roles that a more advanced society demands. Warriors, herdsmen, drovers, stone cutters, hunters, gatherers, forgers, etc. filled villages, and deities blessed each occupation and gave their energies to assist in these necessary pursuits.

Christianity came slowly to Europe over the course of several centuries, but the church found itself fighting a losing battle with the common people's reliance on their old gods and the ways of the Old Religion. Rather than try to overturn the past, the church attempted to overlay it with a Christianized version of the old gods and their myths. What they could not eradicate or assimilate, they diabolized, and what they couldn't diabolize, they twisted to suit their version of the way the universe operated.

Examples of Pagan concepts, holidays, and festivals assimilated and modified by Christianity are numerous. Early Christians found little opposition because they presented to the masses the concept of just one more sun god that fit the form the people were used to worshipping. The god of the Christian church, like the god of the Pagans, was a sun or son, born at the winter solstice of a virgin goddess, and he died and was reborn to serve his people again.

The shrines and sacred groves of European Pagans were covered over with the church's version of deity and the shrines of the new religion. The ease with which this gradual takeover progressed surprises many modern Pagans. Yet all the church did was spend a few centuries giving the people of Europe one more god who fit the archetype they were used to venerating. For the Pagans this was just one more deity, and he was welcome alongside their own.

The Christian church, centered in Rome, found it difficult to erase the pre-Christian festivals and deities from the minds of the people who believed the wheel of the year to be sacred, and that it was a sacrilege not to observe it. What they couldn't dismantle they overlayed with their Christianity, covering sacred wells and mounds and using the archetypal myths of Jesus almost identical to the other sacrificial gods being worshipped throughout Europe.

It was this open acceptance by Pagans of the archetype of the sacrificed king/god, rather than the individual deity, that made it easy for Christianity to become the dominant religion of Europe and gain the strength to enforce obedience to their "one God" by threat of death.

Witchcraft went into hiding, remaining alive the same way it did in the beginning, among small clans and families. Faery tales and myths kept the memory of the old gods alive during the centuries when even appearing to worship outside the Christian church could get you killed.

During the Middle Ages, the wealthy classes developed an interest in magick, particularly in alchemy, an art which seeks to turn base metals into gold. Growing out of the Pagan practices of Egypt and the Middle East, these people were the first ceremonial magicians. They circumvented the death sentence not only because of their high place in society, but because they agreed to serve the kings and queens of the land, and because they used various names for the Judeo-Christian god in their rites. One team of magicians became indispensable at the court of England's Queen Elizabeth I. John Dee and Edward Kelly cast astrological charts to find the best times for their queen or her troops to act, and they developed much of the angelic magick and language that ceremonial magicians still use today.

Fortunately, remnants of the Old Religion survived until it became of interest again in the late nineteenth century, a time when their was also a resurgence of interest in ceremonial magick. Well-educated and influential men were combining the ancient rights of Masonry with

angelic magick and regional mythology to form secret societies—societies from which modern Witchcraft has
drawn many of its tools and rituals.

Somewhere around this time, Wicca was not so much
reborn as it was rediscovered and pieced together from
scraps of mythology and from oral traditions. Like a
phoenix rising from the ashes of fear and oppression,
Witchcraft became accessible once more and soared like a
mighty eagle commanding the skies. The tenet of reincar-
nation was again embraced and, at the roaring start of the
industrial age, these new adherents began to look at
Mother Earth with new eyes and with a deep sense of respect that conjured up a need to protect her. Folklore was
collected by scholars such as Alexander Carmichael and
Sir James Frazer, who produced huge volumes of work we
still rely upon today to catch glimpses of our Pagan and
magical pasts. The Celtic Renaissance, lead by high-born
and wealthy poets such as Ireland's William Butler Yeats,
further fed a desire to learn about the Pagan heritage of
one's own land and cultural heritage.

In the 1950s, after England's repeal of the anti-Witchcraft laws, Great Britain saw a renewed interest in what
many felt was their right: a reclaiming of the indigenous
beliefs of their people. Longtime Witches, such as Sybil
Leek and Gerald Gardner, went public with their beliefs,
drawing new adherents and spawning new Craft traditions.

One well-known student of Gerald Gardner's, Raymond Buckland, is credited with bringing the Gardnerian

version of the Craft to North America and igniting interest among young spiritual seekers. For several decades, Buckland taught and wrote about the changing face of American Witchcraft and earned his place as a respected elder who has been dubbed by some "the grand old man of the Craft."

All these brave Witches, who once had to hide their beliefs from the outside world, began to teach the Old Religion to others; a few formed their own traditions out of history and mythology.

During the counterculture movement of the 1960s, when rejection of authoritarian institutions was the norm among the young, a second wave of attraction to Witchcraft was born. The feminist movement was also alive and well during this decade, and many women found comfort in worshiping a female deity.

Throughout the 1990s and into the twenty-first century, we've seen what we might call the third wave of Witchcraft revival. In spite of the lack of reliable statistics, some researchers and pollsters have found the Craft and its many expressions to be the fastest-growing religious movement in the Western world. The Wiccan and the Wiccan-curious of all ages, genders, and economic backgrounds are seeking out books, videos, music, and mythology to feed their insatiable desire for knowledge.

Praised be the God and Goddess, and praised be those brave practitioners who hid under the cloak of darkness and danger to worship as they chose, who never let the old ways completely die!

a critical eye on craft history

Remember what I said in the first chapter about being a perpetual student and reading with a critical eye? Well, this holds especially true for our history. Lack of knowledge about its history is dangerous to any religion, the Craft included, but widely held misconceptions can be downright deadly. We are only now abandoning many incorrect beliefs. Better research techniques now tell us that we were wrong about many things we believed about the history of the Craft, or, at the very least, the facts we believed were very exaggerated. I have been as guilty of passing these misbegotten ideas along as anyone else. To my everlasting chagrin—a feeling I share with many longtime Witches—I stopped thinking for myself for a few hours, allowing nonsense to replace my common sense and critical-thinking skills.

As the Craft grows into the twenty-first century, it can only benefit from rigorous examination of its history and belief—not to mention from rigorous debunking of misconceptions. One particularly embarrassing fallacy we've done away with is the insistence that more than nine million people died over five centuries of Witch executions—known popularly as "the Burning Times"—until those practices died out in the early eighteenth century. The numbers simply don't make sense in terms of the world's population during those centuries (many scholars now believe the figure to be nearer to fifty thousand[1]), yet for unknown reasons, we accepted this number as a fact for decades. And it is a shame that we did so, because the plight of Witches (or anyone suspected of being a Witch, for that matter) between the fifteenth and eighteenth centuries is horrific enough and needs no exaggeration.

Burning was indeed a common punishment for heresy, and was a popular manner in which to eliminate suspected Witches in Germany. Witches were tortured and executed by a wide variety of cruel and painful means, though.

In England, where Witchcraft was against the laws of a land, hanging was the most common form of capital punishment. It was in the English courts where the test for a Witch was to strip the accused and examine her for a "Witch's teat." This was the place where she suckled Satan, so any women with a wart, mole, liver spot, scar, or pimple was in danger

Dunking was another popular method of testing for a Witch. The Puritans who made the pilgrimage from England to the Massachusetts Bay Colony in the early 1600s came not to practice religious freedom as much as to found a society in which theirs was the only religion. With the Puritans, you couldn't win once the accusation of Witch was placed upon you. Testing a Witch often involved dunking her repeatedly. If she survived the ordeal, she was a Witch and condemned to death by hanging; if she died of drowning or hypothermia, then she was innocent of the charge—but dead all the same.

It's important to seek the facts about the Craft's history and to keep a sharp eye on everything you read, but don't lose your sense of humor or close your mind. Learn now to laugh at your mistakes. If you take yourself too seriously, or if you become too rigid in your thinking, your journey into the Craft will be fraught with petty battles and unseemly arrogance that do nothing to enhance the purpose of being a Witch. Learn from your mistakes and your misbegotten ideas and you'll find a soul-satisfying joy in your spiritual quest. Take yourself too seriously and you not only take the joy out of your faith, but you also diminish your personal growth and become a pain in the rear to others.

ethnic cultures within wicca

Often times you will hear other Witches talk about their "tradition." This refers to a sub-sect of Pagan or Wiccan practice. This is similar to someone saying they are a Christian, but within Christianity there are numerous expressions, or traditions, of worship. A Christian can be a Baptist, a Roman Catholic, or a Lutheran, but he remains a Christian in his basic beliefs. The same is true in Pagan practice, only with greater confusion.

The term "Wicca" as a label for Anglo-Celtic Paganism was coined and made public by the early-twentieth-century Witch Gerald Gardner. Gardner had a tremendous influence on the neo-Pagan movement in the mid-1950s when, after England repealed its anti-Witchcraft laws, he wrote a book outlining the beliefs and practices of his tradition, which he called Wicca. At that time, and until the early 1980s, the term "Wicca" was used almost exclusively to refer to the specific practices of Gardner's followers.

This tradition is now known as Gardnerian Witchcraft or Gardnerian Wicca.

Today there are literally hundreds of traditions or sub-sects of Witchcraft, some that embrace the word "Wicca" in their name, and many that do not. Most often the traditions that use the word "Wicca" will refer to their traditions with a cultural label attached, such as Greco-Roman Wicca, Irish Wicca, Saxon Wicca, Scottish Wicca, etc. Other traditions use the names of their founders or words from their lands of origin that refer to Witches. For example, Streghería is Italian Witchcraft; the word *strega* means "witch" in Italian. Another example is Alexandrian Witchcraft, a tradition founded in the 1960s by one of Gardner's followers, Alexander Saunders.

Each of these traditions has its own set of standards for initiation, and their beliefs about cosmology (creation of all) and eschatology (end of time) will vary. To be considered a Witch of a particular tradition you will have to be initiated into that tradition by someone else within that tradition, after following their specific program of study. This is true whether you have been a practicing Witch for thirty days or thirty years.

making our own history

We cannot hope to reconstruct the precise way Witchcraft was practiced two thousand years ago, nor should we want to. Perhaps the precise ways in which we honor the elements or cast our sacred circles are not identical to the way they were done several millennium ago. This does not invalidate any tradition as a legitimate spiritual path for today's Witches. A religion that doesn't stretch and evolve to match the growth of its adherents soon dies out. It becomes like a stagnant pond, unable to support any life forms except those in the power seats. When the power brokers lose their congregations due to the stagnation, their sect of a faith soon dies.

Endnotes

1. Greer, John Michael. *The New Encyclopedia of the Occult*. (St. Paul: Llewellyn Publications, 2003), pp. 75–78.

a witch's life

There is no such creature as a typical Witch. We come from all strata of society, ethnic backgrounds, and income levels. Where we find our common ground is in the ways we integrate our spirituality into our daily lives.

Unlike religions where the burden of priesthood is performed by an intermediary, Wiccans have no barriers between themselves and their deities other than those they erect themselves. We are each expected to carry our share of the ritual energy, to forge personal relationships with our deities, to behave in an ethical manner, and to do our share of the work at coven meetings or other group gatherings. We are also expected to practice our love for Mother Earth, not just give it lip service. To that end, we leave our ritual sites cleaner than we found them, and often we leave gifts of food for Mother Earth and the creatures who walk upon her face. This is not the same as worshipping nature; instead, it is venerating nature as a tangible sign that the creator of all things is alive and well and dwelling both within us and outside of us.

We go through our lives realizing—just as other faiths proclaim—that we are each created in the image of our deities. We are but microcosmic versions of the macrocosmic power of the universe. Therefore, if deity can create, so can we. Often you'll read or hear this expressed in the couplet,

> As above, so below;
> As within, so without.

Witchcraft acknowledges—even embraces—its metaphysical aspects. We accept that not everything we see is real or that everything real can be seen by us. All religions have their metaphysical aspects in that they urge you to seek out your deities, but not all religions want you to do this for yourself, so they give you a minister, priest, or rabbi to fulfill that role. Witches know the names of many deities, and one to which she is close enough to call her patron. The Witch serves her patron and the patron helps her get to where she needs to be—not always where she wants to be.

Many Pagans enjoy discussing among themselves the many ways in which the universe may work, our place within it, and our relationship with its divine elements. I lost lots of sleep in college staying up until dawn debating all the "what ifs." For these reasons, we often refer to Witchcraft as a "mystery religion." The only way to get where you want to go is taking a few spiritual risks.

As a mystery religion, each individual devises a unique spiritual concept and uses it as a threshold from which to embark on a series of studies transcending those of the current parameters of orthodox science. We seek to dig deeper than society wants us to go, for it is deep within ourselves that the greatest mysteries are discovered. No one should have to tell you that, as science progresses, many things that are now labeled magickal or metaphysical will come to have solid scientific explanations. Most Witches will express the belief that, someday, science will be able to fully explain why and how magick works. So far, it has proven a number of interesting confirmations from our collective beliefs, such as that life cycles are best described in the shape of spiral, like DNA, or that time itself is an illusion which takes us to the outer edge of its reach than draws us back to where we began.

taking time out

Pagans of all traditions go through their daily lives doing many of the same things you do everyday. We have to tend to the needs of our families, go to work or school, endure the demands of unreasonable bosses, poor teachers, frustrated clients, and irate customers. We run errands, pay bills, get stuck in traffic jams, fall ill, and need good food and sleep to stay healthy and strong to face it all day after day. We are people much like you. We just happen to follow a spiritual path that once blanketed the planet and is only now being fully rediscovered and being satisfactorily adapted to fit into modern life.

Once upon a time in Europe—and most anywhere else on the face of the earth—clans and communities took time off from the usual demands of the day to celebrate solar and lunar festivals in much the same way that Christmas is celebrated in North America today. These festivals and feast days could last for as long as a week. Everyone had a role to play and everyone had time to play.

We do share one problem with other minority religions. Today's Wiccans don't always have the luxury of being able to take off from work for our sacred holidays, and many fear losing their jobs if they dared ask. This forces us to do some creative rearranging of our lives to accommodate our spirituality.

If you're a fellow city dweller, as I am, it may take a second pair of eyes for you to find nature and elementals. In town, gardening is harder, and so is finding quiet time. See appendix 5 for books on urban Paganism.

In hunter-gatherer societies, the burden of "making a living" only took a few hours a day, leaving lots of free time to pursue the spiritual. In our modern societies and large cities, making that living can take more than ten hours a day, plus long commutes and errands and appointments that must be squeezed in between other commitments.

If you are a solitary, meaning a Witch who works and worships alone, you have a little more flexibility than if you are part of a coven or study group. You can decide if you feel more in tune with a particular holy day by commemorating it on its eve, on its actual day, or on the day after. When you are alone at night, you can celebrate any Pagan festival from any culture in your devotions and prayers.

Many Wiccans start or end each day with personal devotions to their deities. This is usually done at a small, personal altar on which symbols of the four major elements (to be discussed in detail in the next chapter) are placed. Prayer and meditation follow. Then the Witch will ground his excess energy before heading out of the house to start the day or before retiring to sleep for the night.

meditative consciousness and grounding

Learning to slow your mind and concentrate on your work is an important skill a new Witch needs to develop. This intense focus allows the conscious mind to connect with the subconscious and superconcious minds, and, in doing so, allows information to flow freely from one side of the brain to another so we may use it for magick, ritual, or personal insight.

Meditation can be performed in a variety of ways depending on what you hope to achieve. In its most basic form, meditation is no more than consciously dwelling on a specific symbol or phrase, the latter sometimes referred to as a *mantra*. "Mantra" is Sanskrit for "instrument of thought." It came into Hindustani dialects (and into the Hindu religion) as a word meaning "a sacred hymn," usually one with specific spiritual meaning to the one using it. Essentially, it is a word or phrase repeated over and over to one's self in order to lull the mind into an altered or slowed state of consciousness for the purpose of gaining divine enlightenment.

Altered states of consciousness are necessary biological processes. Without the ability to slow the mind, you would be in manic hyperdrive all the time, unable to relax, read, or even sleep. An altered state of consciousness refers only to the slowing of the cycles per second of your brain. We know this because modern medical equipment can read those cycles to diagnose mood, personality, or sleep disorders. Your altered states occur naturally throughout the day as you read, study, or watch TV, and occur throughout the night as your progress through your natural sleep cycles. The only thing we do differently in mediation is attempt to take control of the process for personal relaxation, centering, and balancing of our inner selves, and for putting ourselves in a receptive state of mind for ritual or magick.

Even if you decide after reading this book, or later on in your studies, that you don't want to be a Witch, learning how to meditate will still have beneficial effects on your mind and body. Those who meditate on a regular basis find relaxation and sleep easier to attain, and they suffer less often from stress-related illnesses such as hypertension and some cancers.

Basic meditation

If you are unfamiliar with the art of meditation, start practicing by following these basic steps:

step 1

Select a symbol or single word on which to focus your attention. It can be a magick symbol, a letter or number, or a word relating to your new spiritual interests. Remember that you will be in a suggestible state of mind, so you want to choose only positive images upon which to concentrate.

step 2

Fix the symbol or word in your mind while thinking of all its ramifications. Words mean different things to different people, and the one you choose can color your meditative experience.

step 3

Get comfortable either sitting or lying down. Only lie down if you think you can stay awake. It won't hurt you to fall asleep while meditating, but you lose most of its benefits that way. You want to be somewhere quiet and private, where you can be sure of not being disturbed for at least fifteen minutes—a half hour is even better. Most meditation sessions last longer, but as a beginner you should aim for ten consecutive minutes of focused thought.

step 4

Relax your body completely, trying not to move unless you feel points of stress or discomfort. Think in terms of putting your body to sleep while your mind remains awake and under your control. You may need to use the standard progressive body relaxation, starting with your toes and working your way up through the top of your scalp.

You don't have to be dead to the world to do successful meditation. You can be conscious of your physical surroundings or not, depending on where you're comfortable and how deep into a meditative state you want to go.

There are four levels of brain activity that can be measured on a brain-scanning machine. The fastest is beta, which corresponds to your normal, waking consciousness. The next level is alpha which corresponds to watching TV or daydreaming. It's also the level of REM sleep, or rapid eye movement sleep, in which dreams occur. This is the minimal level you need to worry about achieving at this time.

The next slowest level is called theta, and it corresponds to a level of sleep in which you are unaware of anything but your sleep state. With practice you can reach this level in meditation and your results will be stronger and your visualizations for magick and ritual will be more powerful.

The lowest level is delta, and this level corresponds with the deep sleep and the unconsciousness levels of brain activity. It is not a state easy to attain in meditation, nor is it necessary. There is no level slower than delta. Below delta is clinical brain death.

step 5

When you feel fully relaxed and at peace, begin to think only of the symbol or word you've chosen to be the focus of your meditation. You may envision it as being static or in motion as long as you think of nothing else.

step 6

If you find your mind wandering away, simply return it to where you want it to be. Don't allow failures to upset you. They occur in all of us occasionally, even after years of experience. Becoming frustrated will only make your efforts more difficult.

Bringing your mind back to where you want it is the beginning of your training in mental discipline, which will help you tremendously in your future Craft endeavors. If after a few months of daily practice you find you still have trouble keeping focused, you might try adding soothing, nonlyrical music, incense, earplugs, or a metronome to help assist your concentration.

At some point you may see symbols "come to life" and rearrange themselves to reveal something to you. This is not the product of a wandering mind, even though you may be equally aware of your meditative world and your physical world at the same time.

In the beginning, you will tire easily. When it becomes too much of an effort to hold the image in your mind, you should allow yourself to become conscious of your physical body once again. Begin to move and stretch, open your eyes, and ground yourself.

Grounding

Grounding is the final step that concludes any metaphysical or magickal endeavor. The idea is to send back into Mother Earth the energy you've drawn up from her. This accomplishes two things. First of all, it anchors your psyche back in the physical world, and, secondly, it takes unused magickal energy from you, energy that would otherwise just hang around, making you feel frazzled, unfocused, or even haunted.

Newcomers tend to gloss over or forget the grounding step until the energy they keep inside starts to attract unwanted astral, or otherworldly, beings or makes them feel crazy. I had both happen in my first year of study. Like so many before me, there were some things I had to learn the hard way. Thinking we can skip the time-tested practices that make Wicca a true craft is not smart.

To ground yourself, place both feet and both palms on the floor or the ground, and visualize all the excess energy leaving your body. Take a few deep breaths, and visualize all the excess leaving you as you exhale. Until you gain some experience at gauging when the process is complete, you would be wise to take a shower or bath after meditation, ritual, divination, or spellwork. As you wash, envision all the excess energy—and any negative energy—being freed from your body, mind, and spirit, and being carried down the drain far away from you. Eventually, you will be able to ground yourself with visualization alone if you don't feel like touching the ground, or if you are in a place where your actions would be frowned upon.

the rede and the threefold law

The highest law I now shall teach,
Mind well your actions, thoughts, and speech;
Many beings can hear and spirits know,
The wickedness you seek not to show.
So turns the wheel from year to year,
Live in their love and have no fear;
This ancient wisdom to you I tell,
As it harms none, do what you will.
Take caution of the next law too,
For all you do comes back to you;
The wheel keeps turning, three times three,
It cannot be fooled nor hidden be.
Walk in harmony, balance, and love,
For as below is as so above;
May your God light shine for all to see,
As you will, so mote it be.

There are few rules governing Witchcraft, which is one reason it is so attractive to independent thinkers. This does not mean we can just do anything we want and excuse it by saying it's part of our religion. Wicca is ultimately a path for those mature enough to embrace total self-responsibility. If you're the sort of person who uses unsupervised time to slack off or indulge in things you know aren't right or might cause harm to someone else, then Witchcraft may not be the religion for you. If, however, you can discipline yourself to work alone, then you may attain great spiritual insights from your efforts.

Each coven and each Witch is an autonomous body, free to determine ritual practices, cultural focuses, rules of order, and how much and for whom acts of magick or healing will be performed. These are cherished rights that in most Western countries are protected by freedom of religion laws. Unfortunately, freedom doesn't always mean tolerance, but we're getting there, little by little.

As a student Witch, the first thing that will test your mind is the fact that you must stop thinking of events in linear time and space, and, instead, think in terms of never-ending cycles or spirals. We have cycles of life, cycles of death and rebirth, cycles of the seasons, cycles of the moon, cycles within our physical bodies, and cycles of energy that correspond to the huge web of existence of which all living things are a part. What we put into these cycles, this wheel of existence, eventually circles back to us carrying with it all the other energies that have been placed upon it after it left us. This is why we must always be conscious of our thoughts, words, and deeds. Witches, Wiccans, and other Pagans do all they can to adhere to this precept, called the Witch's Rede, which can be expressed this way: *As it harms none, do what you will.*

Sometimes this Rede is written in archaic language to make it sound more profound, but all it really means is that we do not have the right to interfere in the free will of any other being, whether it is a being from the animal kingdom, a fellow human, or someone who is of an unseen realm. This includes healing rituals for those who expressly don't want them, and any other "trying to be of help" spells that someone does not give their permission for you to enact.

The penalty for breaking the Rede is expressed in the Craft as the Threefold Law. This law tells us that everything we do comes back to us threefold. Positive energy attracts positive outcomes. Negative energy attracts negative outcomes. This is why the whiners and ne'er-do-wells never get out of their cycle of problems, no matter how much they try or how much help they receive. Their own negativity is being sent out from them onto the wheel of existence, where it attracts more negative energy, and it then comes back to them threefold, only making their problems worse.

This is the way the energy of the universe works, and almost every known religion has a similar rede and a similar concept of retribution for wrongs done to others. In Wicca, this is not used as a scare tactic to make adherents toe the party line, rather it reminds us that we are all connected in spirit on what we call the web of all that is. Each delicate thread of the web holds up another part, so we need all parts at their best to survive.

Later in the book, we'll explore further how magick, ethics, and Wicca are related and why they cannot be separated to avoid the ramifications of the Threefold Law.

magick in wicca

I want to take a moment to mention the role of magick in the Craft since many newcomers are anxious to learn more about this aspect of the Wiccan faith.

As they say in Louisiana, magick is *lagniappe*. It's something extra. A bonus, but not a requirement. Witches use magick when necessary because we acknowledge the natural laws of energy upon which magickal energy is based. You'll find most serious Witches are not in the spell-of-the-moment club. Magick is used when all other avenues have failed us or when we wish to shore up those other avenues with extra personal power. Magick is never required, but its physics and ethics must be understood if you want to be a Witch.

Many newcomers express surprise that magick is often one the last practices they study before their initiations. This is because it is one of the more difficult areas to master since it draws on other skills you will be developing as you go through your year and a day of study—and because it is not the sole purpose of the Craft. Our purpose is that of all religions: the worship of and eventual reunion with our creators.

When we seek to draw energy from the deities and the world they created to enact spells, we call this magick. When we seek to reunite ourselves with our creators, this is called mysticism. Mysticism may come in many guises and be practiced in many ways, but it is the reason for being of any religion, all Pagan faiths included.

Later in this book we'll examine magick and spellcraft and how they work in greater detail. Before we can work spells, we have to understand the nature and use of ritual in Witchcraft.

the power of ritual

Magick is change. Ritual gives us a structure in which to change. Therefore, ritual is a form of magick, and it plays a large role in the life of a Witch.

Ritual's purpose is to turn all areas of the mind—the subconscious, conscious, and superconscious—in a specific direction to achieve a specific desired outcome. The change you seek can be as dramatic as casting a spell to find a new home or as subtle as a change in attitude. It's often been said that each mind is a universe unto itself. What your mind accepts as fact becomes your reality. And, yes, there can be multiple realities, all

41

valid, all real, and all spinning along on the wheel of existence in perfect harmony.

This sounds complex to many newcomers, but it's not. All it takes is practice in working in a ritual state of consciousness, which is really no different from your mental state when you read, watch TV, or meditate.

One of the most appealing things about Witchcraft is that we do not need intermediaries to assist us in our rituals. We recognize that each one of us contains a part of the God and Goddess within, so no intermediaries are needed to connect with the divine. Any witch can connect with the source from which all manifestation is first germinated in the otherworld (the realm of the deities and the source of their divine energy).

Covens and Wiccan study groups are not leaderless, but the leader's role is often one of a facilitator rather than an intermediary. Priests and priestesses never bear the entire ritual burden for any group. Everyone is expected to shoulder her share of the load. Even in groups where there is a well-defined hierarchy, leaders only use their experience to direct the ritual energy. Leaders should be experienced enough to be able to sense when the group has raised magickal energy to its peak, and to direct the group when to let it go toward its goal. They can also help teach you to be the best channel for the divine that you are capable of being.

sacred spaces

Whether you are part of a coven, a study group, or work as a full-time solitary practitioner, you are always free to create your own circles, cast your own spells, and cordon off sacred space, which you can use for any number of reasons.

The circle in which Witches work and worship is a symbol of eternity. It represents the cycles of all that is, was, or ever will be, and it puts the Witch in a realm between realms. Time and space coalesce in sacred circles. Often you won't have any accurate estimation of how much time is passing in the physical world. Wearing a watch is useless, as they tend not to function well within a properly cast circle. Oftentimes you will end your ritual and feel as if you've truly been somewhere else. In fact, you have. Your mind, which is connected with your soul and the essence of the true you, has been elsewhere. There's no mistaking the feeling when you ground your circle; you'll feel similar to the way you do when you've spent a couple nights away from home. You loved your trip, but it's so nice to be home again.

The modern Witches' circle has traditional elemental correspondences that are called upon to assist the ritual or spell being enacted. Be aware that these are by far the most common correspondences and, unless you are being trained to work within a specific tradition that uses uncommon elemental correspondences, you could set yourself up for difficulties later if you deviate from them.

Your ritual state of consciousness can be defined as a manic state of meditation. The cycles per second of your brain waves will slow, but your body may feel as if it's in hyperdrive. This combination creates what some shamans and magicians call the state of divine ecstasy.

Creating your sacred space

When you have at least thirty minutes of uninterrupted time, practice creating your own sacred space by following these steps:

step 1

Spend as much time as you can in mediation before embarking on any ritual. This helps connect all three aspects of your mind so they can work in harmony with your will. It will also help you to purge your mind of random thoughts so you can focus on the task at hand.

You may also wish to do some deep rhythmic breathing, or take a bath or shower with the idea that you are purifying your body and spirit, preparing yourself to be in the presence of, or a channel for, the divine.

If you have the luxury of privacy and a bathtub, take advantage of it and soak away your psychic dirt and mundane worries. You might even want to add scent to the water by tying small sacks of herbs associated with purification. Herbs that fall into that category are hyssop, mugwort, orris, jasmine, lily, and lavender.

step 2

Wear ritual robes if you have them. If not, you may wear loose street clothing or night clothes. If you are in a private space, you may work in a state of ritual nudity referred to as being "skyclad."

The mere act of preparing yourself for ritual will, over time, create triggers in your mind that will turn your mind in the direction you want it to go even before your circle is cast. For example, once you put on your ritual dress, your mind will be automatically triggered to work in a specific way, hopefully the one most advantageous to your goals. Plan now how you want to work in the future, and try to conform to your preritual habits as much as possible.

step 3

Set up an altar close to the middle of your circle area. A simple flat surface of any shape is acceptable. The altar is a microcosm of your circle and provides a center of focus for your rites. It honors your deities, provides a portal for invited spirits, helps raise the vibrational rate in the circle, and gives the elements a tangible presence.

At this point, it's unlikely that you've had time to research and make or buy the ritual tools that represent each element. For now, you might just want to have two white candles on the altar, one each to honor the God and Goddess, whom you will ask to be present at your ritual.

Once you delve deeper into Witchcraft, you will accumulate ritual tools that correspond with the four cardinal directions: east, west, north, and south. These are used to house elemental energy for use in magick or ritual and to provide a place for each element to reside on your altar. Do not think you have to have them all right now, or that you ever have to have them. Magick is always within the magician. Our props are merely the catalysts we use to focus upon our goals. They may share energies that resonate with a specific spell or ritual goal, but a skilled Witch can enact magick and ritual with no tools other than her own mind and body.

Traditional tools for the elements are numerous and, in some cases, overlapping. Among the most commonly chosen are:

- **East and Air:** Athame (a doubled-edged ritual blade), sword, wand, book, pen, letter opener, feather, pentacle, wood, mortar and pestle.

- **South and Fire:** Candle, wand, blade, red or orange stone, pyrite, gold.

- **West and Water:** Chalice, cup, bowl, wine, water, juice, silver, coral, stones with holes in their centers, seaweed, seashells.

- **North and Earth:** Crystals, stones, salt, ashes, ground, grain, berries, fruit.

- **Center and Akasha:** (*Akasha* is the Sanskrit word for spirit, the element that unites and empowers all the others to work in harmony.) Sometimes an egg, egg timer, or cloak is used to symbolize akasha, but most often the fifth element is called upon without the aid of a specific tool.

Some traditions use the additional directions of above and below to further represent the element of sprit. Others assume spirit is present at all times and do not make a separate call to invite spirit into their circle. With practice you will discover which way works best for you.

step 4

Walk the perimeter of your circle, drawing up energy from the earth to create it, moving slowly clockwise, or what we call *deosil* (pronounced JEZ-el) or "sunwise." This is the direction of increase, gathering, gain, positive action, or manifestation. As you walk the perimeter, feel the sphere of energy engulfing your sacred space, growing stronger and vibrating at a high rate.

As you walk, visualize energy being drawn up from Mother Earth beneath you, surrounding your circle area in a protective blue-white light of energy. You may make one pass around the circle or more. You may choose more because you feel it's necessary to make your circle its strongest, or to be in keeping with the sacred number of a particular cultural tradition. For example, the Celts, among many others, held the number three and its multiple of nine sacred, and many Celtic-based traditions employ these numbers whenever possible.

Also, don't be tempted to skimp on the circle casting to get to the "real" stuff. As I've said, the ritual that comes before your ritual is ritual. That's not gobbledygook but a way of allowing a repeated spiritual action to tell your deep mind that a change is about to take place. This is necessary as you grow in your Witch's skills because, over time, your power will grow, and you'll need your basic skills more than ever.

I learned this lesson the hard way when a friend and I were beginners. We were anxious to try scrying (gazing at an object, often a bowl of liquid, for prophetic visions) and something quite hideous and wicked attempted to use our scrying pool as a portal because we had not cast our circle properly.

Later, when you ground your circle, you will move in a counterclockwise direction to represent decrease, banishment, loss, negative action, and dismantling. As you walk in this direction—which we sometimes call *widdershins*—you will envision your circle dissipating and sinking into the ground below you.

Do not buy into the fallacy many newcomers adopt that counterclockwise is the same as evil, or that doing anything in a counterclockwise motion bodes ill. One of our Wiccan mysteries is that there is no ultimate negative or positive energy anywhere in the universe. Sometimes a negative action yields a positive result, such as when you're trying to banish a bad habit or overcome a fear. Only the intent of the one performing the spell or ritual determines if an action is truly negative, as in wicked or harmful to others.

Your circle serves three important functions:

1. It provides a space safe from capricious, unpredictable, or negative beings who might be attracted to the energy you raise.

2. It creates a world between worlds—a sphere of the sacred—that puts you at the center of all time and space.

3. The circle's boundaries hold in all the energy you raise and keep it circulating until you're ready to send it off towards its goal with visualization and physical gestures.

step 5

You may begin evoking the elements with any direction you choose. This is often dictated by tradition or by the purpose of your ritual. Using the Celts again as an example, many of their adherents start their quarter calls in the west, the traditional direction of the otherworld where the deities dwell. The majority of Wiccans gravitate toward beginning in the east, the direction the sunrise and new beginnings. Others start at a different point depending upon the season or the purpose of their rituals. For example, a Midsummer ritual might be started in the south, the home of the sun, while a circle cast for a spell for money might be started in the north, the direction associated with home, wealth, and abundance.

Move clockwise, stop at each cardinal point, and invite—never demand!—the presence of the elements and their attendant elemental rulers. These are sentient beings and deserve respect for their goodwill. Respect them, and they can assist you in any spell or ritual you chose. Abuse their goodwill, and they can work against you.

Many beginner's Witchcraft books give you complete texts for rituals with a variety of evocations, or "quarter calls," some very elaborate and others very simple. Your quarter calls might sound something like these:

Spirits of the east and air, realm of communication and intellect, ruled by the sylphs of air who dance upon the four winds, I call you to this circle to join me in [insert purpose of your ritual here]. Merry meet and welcome.

Spirits of the south and fire, realm of courage, passion, and lust, ruled by the salamanders of flame, I call you to this circle to join me in [insert purpose of ritual here]. Merry meet and welcome.

Spirits of the west and water, realm of peace, love, and mysteries, ruled by the undines of the waters who dance upon the waves, I call you to this circle to join me in [insert purpose of ritual here]. Merry meet and welcome.

Spirits of the north and earth, realm of the home, of abundance, prosperity, and healing, ruled by the gnomes of the woodlands, I call you to this circle to join me in [insert purpose of ritual here]. Merry meet and welcome.

step 6

The next step is to call upon your deities. Until you become used to working with a specific pantheon and develop relationships with various aspects of the divine, just use the terms "God and Goddess" or "Lord and Lady" when referring to or calling upon the deities.

Go to your altar, where you should have the two unlit candles, and invite the presences of your deities. It doesn't matter whether you call the God or the Goddess first. Almost everyone has an opinion about the order. Use what feels right to you. The evocation of the deities might sound like the following:

Blessed be the Goddess, the mother of all. I ask your loving presence be at this circle now. I evoke you in all your glory, beauty, and ask your blessing on my work. No matter how pressing my physical or emotional needs, never let me forget that my objective is reaching your loving arms once again so that I may be what I am, a part of you. Blessed be and welcome, my Lady.

Blessed be the God, the father of all. I ask that your strength of presence be at this circle now. I evoke you in all your glory, courage, and bounty, and ask your blessing on my work. No matter how pressing my physical or emotional needs, never let me forget that my objective is reaching your strong arms once again so that I may be what I am—a part of you. Blessed be and welcome, my Lord.

As you call upon the deities, you may light a candle on your altar to represent the flame of their presence. If you're not used to working with fire in a ritual state of mind, be extra cautious. It's easy to become distracted by your rites, or to fool yourself into thinking that this safe space you have carved out of the ether will protect you from your own carelessness. It won't. Never leave a flame unattended, even a magickal one, even if it seems steady or is globed.

Make sure your candles are in sturdy containers that rest steadily on your altar and, if they do happen to tip over, they won't do a header into a container of potpourri or your drapes. You also don't want to be dragging your sleeves through the flames as you work, so position candles with forethought as to how your ritual will proceed. Performing a sacred act does not protect against human stupidity.

You have now either opened or closed your circle, depending upon which terminology you like best. Some Witches call casting the circle closing it, as in closing off the space from mundane space, then they open it when there're done. Others open the circle when they cast it, separating it in time and space from the mundane worlds and opening it to the otherworld. I prefer the second terminology, but either is correct.

Your elementals are present to assist you and you have the attention of the God and Goddess of all creation.

step 7

Your next task is to raise psychic or magickal energy for whatever ritual you have in mind.

I will now divulge another one of the so-called secrets or mysteries of Witchcraft: never, never, never use your own energy as you work through a spell or ritual. All this will do for you is drain the reserves you need to stay strong, balanced, and healthy. Instead, you obtain your energy from one of four sources:

1. You draw it up from Mother Earth.

2. You draw it down from the otherworld deities.

3. You pull it in from one or more of your catalysts, such as an herb or gemstone.

4. You raise it within you by dancing, drumming, or otherwise charging the atmosphere around you with kinetic energy, and channel it through yourself toward your goal.

Using your sacred space

Now you have cast your circle. You've evoked the elements and your deities. You have raised energy so that the potential to make magick is present. Now what do you do?

enact a ritual

You can use the space for working and worshiping in safety and harmony with the higher spirits and deities of the universe.

Rituals can be enacted for a variety of reasons, including:

- Seasonal celebrations
- Lunar ceremonies

- Lifecycle events and commemorations

- Praise of the deities

- Offerings of thanksgiving

- Magick you want enacted in a ritualized format

- To invoke or evoke a deity

- To meditate in a balanced environment

- To work divinations within a safe space

For your first ritual you may want to try something simple like the World Tree meditation. This is a common and popular meditation performed by Witches at all levels of skill and experience. The concept behind it is that the World Tree of mythological origin is the center of the universe; it's the axis on which the universe spins. Its roots are the past, your past lives, and the lineage of your ancestors. The trunk is you, standing strong at the epicenter of creation. Your arms will raise high above your head, stretching for eternity into the void. This is the future, your future selves, and your descendants.

Stand with your arms reaching out above your head and imagine they are the branches of the tree reaching high into the sky above you, as if reaching for the world of the divine. Plant your feet firmly beneath you and envision roots growing from them and sinking deep into the sacred soil of Mother Earth. You are now like the World Tree of mythology, one that links past, present, and future, and underworld, living world, and otherworld.

As you slowly work through this meditation, feel the energy of all time, space, and beings of goodwill flowing through you, some sinking into the past and others reaching for the future.

When you feel you've gotten all you can out of this ritual for now, lower your arms, and slowly draw in your roots and branches until your mind and body feel fully back within your circle.

Grounding Your Sacred Space

When you are ready to ground your circle, you will work in reverse order from the way your opened it. A few Witches still have an irrational fear of doing *anything* in a counterclockwise motion, and will dismiss the elements in the same order in which they call upon them. Logically, though, if you call something clockwise, thinking in terms of creation, you would have to do something counterclockwise to perform an act of deconstruction.

If you take nothing else away from this chapter, please let it be that nothing is inherently good or evil. Only the intent of the Witch doing the work makes that distinction.

step 1

Starting in the quarter that faces the direction of the last element you evoked, begin the process of dismissing the elements.

At this point it's important to make an observation about semantics. We use a lot of words in Witchcraft because there are just no good ones to describe a process that must be experienced to be fully understood. If you continue on with Craft studies, you'll find this expressed in an old adage that says these things are "That which can never be told." This has a lot less to do with keeping secrets than it does with the fact that words cannot always transmit to beings in this world the experiences of another world, a realm populated with spirit beings and operating under a set of rules with which you may not be familiar or comfortable.

When we say we dismiss the elements, what we are really saying is that we let them know our rites have ended and they are free to go. As you go to each cardinal point of your circle, your quarter dismissals might sound something like this:

> **Gnomes of the sacred element of earth,** I thank you for standing watch over the northern borders of my circle this night and for lending your stabilizing energies to my [insert reason for casting circle]. You are free to go at your will. Thank you. Merry part, and merry meet again.

> **Undines of the sacred element of water,** I thank you for standing watch over the western border of my circle this night and for lending your loving energies to my [insert reason for casting circle]. You are free to go at your will. Thank you. Merry part, and merry meet again.

> **Salamanders of the sacred element of fire,** I thank you for standing watch over the southern

border of my circle this night and for lending
your passionate energies to my *[insert reason for
casting circle]*. You are free to go at your will.
Merry part, and merry meet again.

Sylphs of the sacred element of air, I thank
you for standing watch over the eastern border
of my circle this night and for lending your ra-
tional energies to my *[insert reason for casting
circle]*. You may leave at your will. Thank you.
Merry part, and merry meet again.

step 2

Next, you will dismiss the deities. The same rule about
semantics applies, even more so in this case. Witches do
not order around their deities. We ask their presences as a
favor to us, we are grateful for their attention, and we re-
lease them with thanks and love.

Again, there is no set rule as to whether you dismiss the
God or Goddess first. Your parting words might sound like
this:

Blessed be the Lord of all. Thank you for the
gift of your presence at this circle, for your protection, your blessings, and your assistance.
Unto all realms I shout my thanks. Hail and
farewell until we merry meet again. So mote
it be.

Extinguish the God candle.

Blessed be the Lady of all. Thank you for the gift of your presence at this circle, for your protection, your loving mother's care of my needs, and your assistance. Unto all realms I shout my thanks. Hail and farewell until we merry meet again. So mote it be

Extinguish the Goddess candle.

Note the lines "so mote it be" at the end of each call. This is a phrase you'll hear a lot in Witchcraft. It's simply archaic English that has been used in the Craft since who knows when. "Mote" does not mean "might" or "maybe," but is a word for "must." By uttering this sentence in a spell or ritual, we are stating our belief that what we will is manifest.

For those of you who are skittish about that confident phrase, the Hebrew word *amen* means the same thing. Depending on how you were raised, you probably said amen hundreds of times with no ill effects. Ask any rabbi and he or she will tell you the translation is the almost the same as the Witches' one. "Amen" means "so be it."

step 3

Starting at the cardinal point where you began dismissing the elements, walk your circle counterclockwise to ground it. Visualize and feel it sinking back into Mother Earth as you walk its boundaries either one or three times. You may walk around again and again if you need to, until you feel the energy you raised is grounded. In time, you will be able to sense the presence of this energy more easily and you will be confident of your efforts with fewer passes around the circle.

Some Witches like to make a statement or some kind of noise at this point—something to signal to the mind and to any beings still present, that your rite has ended. This helps bring your mind back into the mundane world. Statements such as "the rite is done" or "the circle is open but unbroken" are often used. Others ring bells or loudly shout words from a special mantra. The choice of what you do is up to you. Do whatever makes you feel the world of form and spirit are separate once more. You do not want one bleeding into the other or you'll have a portal through which anything can pass. You may find yourself with a house full of bothersome astral entities if you skimp on this step.

step 4

The last step is the all-important one of grounding yourself. As mentioned in the previous chapter, place your feet and palms on the floor or earth, and mentally discharge any residual energy from the ritual into Mother Earth.

Ritual completed

Your head should now be clear, and you should feel as if you've just made a journey from one place to another. You're a little tired, but also exhilarated, charged with the energies of balance, inner harmony, and the blessings of all that is sacred.

The next step is to put ritual energy to practical use, which is where we're going in chapter 5.

what witches do: the sabbats

When a Witch hears the word "ritual," it often resonates within her as being synonymous with the celebrations of the solar year, or what we call the wheel of the year. It's not that this is the only reason for enacting a ritual—not even close—but the celebration of the turning of the wheel of the solar year is a strong ritual theme that echoes across all our traditions in some form or another.

In most traditions of western European-based Witchcraft, the eight solar festival dates are referred to as *sabbats*. The root of the word is from an ancient Greek word, *sabatu*, meaning "to rest or pause," and is the same word from which the English word "sabbath" and the Hebrew *shabat* are derived.

Those of you who are used to saying the word "sabbath" in English usually pronounce "sabbat" with an accent on the first syllable. Those of you with a Jewish background who are used to saying the Hebrew word *shabat* tend to accent the last syllable, the same way the Hebrew equivalent is accented. Either pronunciation is correct, but it's most common to hear the accent on the first syllable.

Deep in the Pagan past, these solar holidays marked two important parts of the year:

1. They were a reflection of the eternal lifecycle of the God and Goddess as they worked themselves through the year.

2. They punctuated any agricultural or herding culture's annual turning points.

The two equinoxes and two solstices are sabbats and, for astrological reasons, always fell on predictable dates. The four crossquarter points, the other four sabbats in between the equinoxes and solstices, however, were not always fixed as they are in our modern practice. They allowed for flexibility depending on the precise time of the planting, harvesting, and animal birthing.

It was not until the late Middle Ages that these cross quarter days were firmly fixed. As Christianity spread over Europe, the community festivals were taken over by the church as feast days for specific saints, or they were used as times for community fairs, where goods were bought and sold and a general carnival atmosphere reigned. It was through these fairs that many of the old sabbat customs were kept and handed down to the next generation. Games seemed harmless enough to the church, which was blissfully unaware they were contributing to keeping cherished Pagan traditions alive.

Even today, in modern Celtic countries, these county or borough festivals attract many visitors who come not just to watch or engage in the trading of animals, crafts, and competition, but also the ancient games. Ireland has many of these, most of them now named after saints. Scotland has its annual Highland Games, and the idea of an annual cultural fair was revived in Wales nearly a century ago.

the eight sabbats of witchcraft

These eight festivals, spaced about six weeks apart throughout the cycle of the solar year, are major holy days in Witchcraft. They are times when covens, study groups, and solitaries are expected to acknowledge the turning of the wheel, to honor the deities as they change throughout the year, and to give thanks for the cycle of the seasons. They are also times of personal devotion and times to reconnect yourself with your creator.

At this point a lengthy, memorized ritual is beyond your grasp, but there are some simple rituals or devotions you can use to emotionally connect with the seasonal energies inside or outside of a circle (as was shown in chapter 4).

Don't worry about "doing anything wrong." If your intent is sincere, focused on worship, and open to new experiences and feelings, you can't make a major mistake.

Samhain (October 31)

Non-Witches, or "Cowan" as they are sometimes called, have a whole mixed bag of silly ideas about what Witches do, especially on the night they know as Halloween. While it is one of our major sacred days (the other being Beltane), there is nothing sinister about it, nor anything so off the wall that should titillate the masses as it seems to do. Not a year goes by without some coven being intruded upon by people who just want to see what hideous rites will be enacted.

The late Sybil Leek, a hereditary Witch from England, wrote in her book *The Complete Art of Witchcraft* that, on one Halloween, a woman broke into her Florida hotel room and refused to leave until she saw whatever Sybil planned to do that night.

The roots of Samhain (pronounced SOW-in, "sow" rhymes with "cow") come from deep in the Celtic past, and are not very thrilling as a spectator sport. The Celtic new year began on the eve of Samhain, or what we know today as All Hallows Eve. Now fixed on October 31, this date could have been celebrated up to two weeks later depending upon how soon the last of the harvest was ready to be gathered in. In some British traditions, November 7 is referred to as the Old Samhain.

Samhain was not only an acknowledgment of the final harvest, but was the night when the God of the old year died, not to be seen again until his rebirth at the winter solstice.

It was considered the worst of luck to take the last piece of the harvest from the fields or trees. Something should always be left to keep the land connected with its produce throughout the long winter to come, and to insure that the Gods and Goddesses of death and regeneration have some marker to follow back in the spring.

Samhain is the night when the veil separating the worlds of spirit and form is at its thinnest, and the souls of our ancestors may pass freely into our world to join in the sabbat celebration. Altars are usually decorated with mementoes of those who have passed before and with harvest items such as apples, pumpkins, turnips, and berries.

The aspects of deity that rule at Samhain are the crone aspect of the Goddess and the Lord of the Hunt. These aspects will have different names depending upon which culture you draw for your personal mythology, but their archetypal functions remain consistent.

The Crone Goddess is the older woman, wise but stern, giving while exacting a price. She is a teacher of tough lessons, but those lessons are always in the best interest of the student. She is not to be feared, for she is the same mother Goddess who gave us life in summer. She is merely old now and can share her knowledge with us, if we stop to listen to her. She is symbolized by the wise old owl who travels by night but is not blinded by darkness.

The Lord of the Hunt is an underworld aspect of the God, who rides upon the night air with his horses and hounds. He seeks souls to take back with him to the underworld. This sounds frightening, but it isn't always. When it's time to die, wouldn't you like a caring God to escort you? The Lord of the Hunt also rounds up lost souls who cannot find the way to the world of spirit, or who do not realize they have died, or who are afraid to leave the familiar for something unknown.

The notion that there is anything evil or Satanic about Samhain is ridiculous. Satan is a construct of Christian theology, and it has no meaning for Witches. This is not a celebration of death, but a celebration of the cycles that bring growth and transformation of the spirit. What our Samhain rituals remind us of is that it is from death that life emerges. Like the caterpillar in his cocoon, death is a respite between life and rebirth.

Another custom carved out of the Pagan past is trick-or-treating. Bread foods are often favorites of the deities and other spirits, so they are ones most often still given as Samhain offerings. After Halloween became All Soul's Day on the church calendar, it became customary for children in England to go door to door asking for soul-cake donations for their altars. Eventually this evolved into the sugar-gathering spree that is modern trick-or-treating.

beginner's samhain ritual

As you did in chapter 4, you will need only two unlit candles on your altar at this time. Don't worry about collecting or making lots of magickal tools until you grow familiar enough with the rituals to know intuitively which ones you want and which work best for you. We're all different and so are our affinities.

Samhain altars are customarily adorned with photographs of loved ones who have already crossed over into the realm of spirit. If you don't have photos, you can use an item passed down to you or some symbol of your ethnic heritage, even if that symbol is only a book on its history and language.

Call out loud the names of your beloved dead. You can even make a blanket call to, for example, all the innocents killed during the Burning Times, or all innocents who died through acts of terrorism, or all who perished in a natural disaster, or through domestic violence. Pet spirits may also be honored.

In many Witchcraft traditions it is customary to call out loud the names of those who have passed over into spirit, and to ring a bell as you give your roll call. These may be family members or any others in spirit you wish to honor. The origins of this custom are hazy, but there are two prominent theories. One is that the bell's tolling brings a higher vibration to the circle, one comfortable and compatible with that of the spirits. The second is that it chases away lesser spirits whom you do not want using your ritual as a portal.

You may speak to your ancestors and ask them to be with you in the year to come or to go with the deities who will take them where they want to go.

Once you become attuned to the presence of spirits, you'll find some occasionally stopping in just to see how you're getting along. This is most likely to happen during the dark part of the year, usually from the autumn equinox through a few weeks past Yule.

Remember, spirits are sentient beings, and you should not violate their free will unless you just cannot tolerate sharing your living space with them. I admit it's discomfiting at first to know another being is moving about your home unseen, but if its someone who loved you in life, he or she could be a comforting, protective presence.

My beloved little sheltie passed over in February 2002 at the age of fourteen; yet come September, I could still feel him near me. I awoke several times to hear his tags jingling as he trotted down the hallway. I could feel his feet stumbling across my ankles to the other side of the bed just as he used to do when he was a young dog and could make the leap up to the bed without my assistance. I know he comes to offer me comfort when I'm feeling low, and probably to reassure me that he is fine in his spirit body, which apparently restored his youth.

When you are ready to end your ritual, thank your deities for coming, extinguish their candles, and ground your circle and then yourself.

Yule or Midwinter (December 21 or 22)

The winter solstice is the New Year's of Norse and Teutonic Pagans. The Old Norse word *jul* literally means "wheel," as in the ever-turning wheel of the year. In most of the Teutonic traditions, the Yule celebration is a twelve-day event, culminating on Twelfth Night in the first week of January.

If all this sounds more like a Christmas custom than a Pagan one, remember again that it was the church that had to make its new mythology appealing to the people of Europe who'd been worshiping and celebrating the old ways for centuries. In the lives of the poor, these festivals dates were eagerly anticipated, not only as holy days, but as a chance to gather with friends and family and take a break from the work of providing for a family or community.

The church could not compete with the allure of Yule, so it merely laid its own veneer of legends atop of what was already accepted practice. Decorated evergreen trees originated with the Teutonic or Saxon Pagans. The tree symbolized eternal life because, unlike other trees in the forest, it never lost its foliage in winter. The candlelight and foods that adorned the tree represented the desire of the people to have the sun return to them on this, the longest night of the year. The food was a sacrifice, a wish that all the tribe would survive throughout the long winter.

In England, the Yule log harkens back to the days of the Druids when the oak was sacred. Oak is a hard wood that burns hot and slowly in the hearth. Like the candlelight on the Saxon evergreens, the Yule log was, in its infancy, an act of magick to lure back the sun.

The Celtic tradition marks Yule in a slightly different way. Their name for the sabbat, Midwinter, comes from the fact that the Celtic winter begins six weeks earlier, on Samhain. Winter ends six weeks after Yule on the sabbat of Imbolg. Therefore, the date we acknowledge today as the start of the winter season was, for the Celts—and those modern Pagans who follow Celtic paths—the midpoint of the winter season, hence Midwinter.

On the solstice night, the God is born to his virgin mother. This is the start of their never-ending lifecycles, which continue throughout the year. The God is son, lover, father, and consort to the eternal Goddess from whose womb all life is born.

It's worth mentioning that the original meaning of the word "virgin" is notably different from its current English usage, referring to a female who has not yet engaged in sexual intercourse. The term originated in Greco-Roman Paganism when a *virgo intactus* was a woman who was whole and complete unto herself. She needed no mate or family to make her whole. Often she was a priestess, one free to take or leave as many lovers as she chose.

Most group rituals will reenact the seasonal battle for supremacy between the archetypes known as the Oak King and the Holly King. The Oak King is the divine ruler of the waxing year and will be victorious in his battle, and the Holly King will die. In truth, they are two faces of the same being, but only one aspect may be with us at any time during the year. Note the white beard of age and the sprig of holly sported on Santa Claus' cap. He embodies the Holly King who is soon to leave us to the rule of his other half, the Oak King.

For those who grew up loving Christmas traditions, please know that you never have to give them up just because you choose Paganism as your path. Many Pagans have tree-trimming parties for their Yule Tree, light Yule Logs, feast on eggnog and cookies, and sing and dance. Those were Pagan customs long before they were adopted by Christianity.

beginner's yule ritual

Again, start with only your two unlit candles. Be cautious about putting seasonal decorations on the same altar with an open flame. Evergreen can dry out quickly and become extremely flammable. Instead of evergreens, you might prefer to use more candles of any style or size you choose. You may also use lanterns, penlights, or any other objects that can illuminate your ritual area.

After you cast your circle and evoke the elementals (see page 44), invite the virgin Goddess and her newborn son, the Sun King, to your circle. If you find this uncomfortable, you can always just ask the God and Goddess to be present. The main concept of this ritual is to welcome the sun's returning to warm the earth. (Please be conscious of your sleeves, hems, pets, children, draperies, or any other flammable items, and never leave a burning candle unattended, even for a moment.) You may wish to chant a short rhyme, or you may wish just to call back the sun with extemporaneous words. As you do this, you may light all the candles, lanterns, etc. that are around you to symbolize the sun as it grows from its shortest appearance at Yule to its longest appearance at the summer solstice.

Stand facing east, the direction of the rising sun, and call upon it to return to you, to warm the earth once more.

When you are finished with this ritual, thank your elements, and ground the circle and yourself.

Imbolg (February 2)

Also known as Imbolc, Oilmec, or Candlemas, this sabbat is another that is Celtic in origin. Falling on February 2, it corresponds to Ireland's Feast of St. Bridget—a Christian disguise for the goddess Brighid—and to Groundhog Day in North America.

The word *imbolg* is said to come from an old Gaelic term meaning "ewe's milk." This is the season when ewes began lactating, meaning they will soon to give birth to lambs. What better harbinger of the spring and renewal could be given to winter-weary people than the thought of lambing season being just ahead?

Because candle lighting (to symbolize the slowly waxing sun) was a major part of the ritual of this sabbat, the term *Candlemas*, or "mass of candles," is another name for the sabbat. Often, in group rituals, a young Pagan woman will wear of crown or ring of lighted candles on her head. This was a Scandinavian Yule custom that came into the Irish Witchcraft practices of Yule sometime after the tenth century, when Viking invaders populated much of the Emerald Isle and intermarried with the local women.

Imbolg is the beginning of the spring season. Even though snow and frost may still blanket the ground, the sun—like the young God he represents—is growing stronger each day. The virgin Goddess is the nurturer at this sabbat, her young breasts full of milk to nourish her young.

beginner's imbolg ritual

Start as usual with your two unlit candles to represent your God and Goddess. Cast your circle and summon the elements (see page 44). Imbolg rituals include the lighting of more candles to represent the waxing of the sun. They also include the blessing and eating of dairy foods, as well as the celebration of the life of the strong, young God and his virgin mother.

To honor the young God and his virgin mother, consider dancing in a spiral formation. It is believed that spiral dancing has been used since prehistory to represent the cycles of time and creation. With the discovery of DNA, the molecular spirals that carry the genetic coding from which we are each created as a unique individual, modern Craft practitioners are embracing the spiral symbol as a representation of our belief in cycles of time and life.

Close you circle as usual and then ground yourself.

Ostara or the Spring Equinox (March 21)

Rebirth, renewal, and regeneration are the themes of Ostara, the sabbat that falls on the spring, or vernal, equinox. Like Yule and Christmas, Ostara shares many symbols and practices with Easter, the Christian holy day which was overlaid on the Pagan festival that could not be eradicated. Even the word "Easter" is derived from Ostara's Teutonic name, "Eostre."

Falling around the time of the old Roman New Year of March 25, spring has been viewed as the season of many kinds of renewals: spiritual, physical, and emotional. The universal symbol of this time of rebirth has always been the humble egg.

Eggs not only represent the potential for new life but give tangible evidence of the equinox. Hens will not lay eggs until their retinas are stimulated with at least twelve hours of light. We can reproduce that environment on modern factory farms, but not so long ago, we had to rely on Mother Nature to provide the twelve hours of light, the light we get from Ostara until the autumn equinox.

Many modern Witches like to use natural dyes to color Ostara eggs. Almost any book on basic Wicca or on the sabbats will teach you how this works. (See appendix 5 for a list of some specific titles.) They are more difficult to color by this method, but I feel every Witch should try it once just to see what happens.

At Ostara, the God and Goddess are envisioned as healthy young adults. Like the warming earth beneath our feet, the warmth of newly discovered sexual awakenings is rousing in our deities. In Pagan group rituals, mating games such as spin the bottle are perennial favorites.

beginner's ostara ritual

Forget the confinement of your ritual circle and move outdoors to welcome spring. On your altar, you may wish to put some brightly colored eggs, which you can leave out later for the animals that are awakening from their winter's hibernation—just as the Goddess of the earth as been sleeping and is now being aroused.

Take a walking stick, cane, staff, long wand, shillelagh, or any other object that you can use to rouse the earth to wakefulness. Walk outside and stop whenever the mood strikes you and tap the ground three times. If others are with you, have them bang pots and pans, blow whistles, or make any other commotion you like. As you walk around the ground, you may sing or chant something like:

> Mother Earth awake to us,
> Or we shall continue to make a fuss;
> Once more it's time to rise and shine,
> Renewing life so lush and fine.

Honor your God and Goddess as youthful and a little sensual. They are awakening to one another as the earth is awakening.

When you conclude your ritual and welcome the return of light from the half year of darkness, you may close the circle and ground.

Beltane (May 1)

> *Hurray, hurray, it's the first of May,*
> *Outdoor mating starts today!*

Many North American teenagers know that verse in one of its many versions, usually the randier ones. It calls to our atavistic instincts, somewhere in our collective, primal memory, we recognize May 1 as a day of sexual license.

Nothing could be more fitting than the randy ram symbolizing this sabbat, which celebrates the sacred union of the God and Goddess—the cosmic sex act that brings all creation into being.

Also spelled "Bealtaine," and celebrated in Germany as *Walpurgisnacht*, Beltane marks the start of the Celtic summer. A bright balefire or sacred bonfire would be burned at the center of the village and all fires in the homes would be lit from this source. Often two balefires were built close together so cattle could be driven between them to protect their milk from being stolen by the faeries, who are especially active during the Beltane and Midsummer months.

At Beltane, the deities have realized their full sexual potential, their ability to procreate. They are united in sacred marriage, and our rituals reflect this union from which all creation will come. The most sacred of the rituals is known as the Great Rite.

The Great Rite is symbolic of the sexual union of the deities. It is usually performed by a priest and a priestess, who personify the deities. The priestess holds a chalice, symbolic of the womb of the mother Goddess, and the priest holds the ritual blade, a phallic symbol. When the two are united, it is representative of the sacred marriage of the God and Goddess.

Another symbol of sacred marriage is that May basket. Like the chalice, it represents the fertility of the Goddess. Items placed into the basket are placed there to germinate and grow. Ostara eggs are often placed in baskets to symbolize the fecundity of the divine couple.

The Maypole dance, in which ribbons are interwoven along a tall, flower-topped pole, is not an uncommon sight, even in the mainstream. For we Pagans, it has many meanings:

1. The pole is the phallus of the God.

2. The braiding of the pole is the vaginal canal of the Goddess.

3. The white ribbons, usually handled by women, represent the virgin Goddess.

4. The red ribbons, usually handled by men, represent her initiation into sexual womanhood.

Ultimately, the dancing of the Maypole represents the impregnation of the earth with this sacred symbol.

beginner's beltane ritual

Flowers and eggs are the most common altar decoration, but, as with the other beginner's sabbat rituals, all you really need at this time are two white candles.

If you have a double-edged blade and a chalice or wine glass, you may wish to try the Great Rite yourself. In it, play both the role of God and Goddess, and unite yourself in the bonds of sacred marriage, thus fertilizing animals, plants, and people.

Litha or Midsummer (June 21 or 22)

Midsummer, or the summer solstice, is the start of the summer season on the Western calendars, but, for the Celts, it marked the midway point of the three-month summer period, hence the name "Midsummer." On the continent, the solstice was known as Litha, a celebration to honor the sun God—and sometimes a sun Goddess—at the peak of his potency.

The Holly King and the Oak King again do battle, just as they did at midwinter, only this time the Holly King is victorious, as the solar years starts to wane.

Other Litha rituals include leaving libations for the faeries, gathering sacred herbs, and burning balefires, over which lovers may leap to signify their commitment to one another in the coming year.

beginner's litha ritual

For this ritual you may wish to forgo the altar and cast your sacred space and evoke your deities alone outside, where you watch the sun rise on its longest day of the year.

Offer praises to the Earth Mother, pregnant now with the coming fall's harvest. Rejoice in your sun God riding high in the sky at the peak of his power.

Remain outdoors as much as is practical for your today, and try to be outside to witness the miracle of the golden sunset. After tonight, the sun will begin to wane and with it, the God's potency.

If you have cast a circle, ground it and yourself in the usual manner.

Lammas (August 1 or 2)

Also known by its Irish name, *Lughnasadh*, "Lammas," comes from a Latin word for the first of the year's harvests, that of grains, and literally means "bread mass." It falls on either August 1 or 2, depending upon your tradition.

In almost every known culture, the threshing house has been a sacred place. The threshold became a symbol of transition, separating one season from another, and the blessing of abundance from the despair of hunger. This is where and why the modern wedding custom of carrying a new bride over the sacred portal of her new home was born. She was carried so she would be symbolically transferred to another realm of being without her footsteps marking the way. Instead, she flies wraithlike, as does the spirit of the Goddess she represents in her new union. As with the threshing house, all houses have doors, and doors represent transition and demarcate a place in between worlds where magick and connection to the divine is much easier to achieve.

Offerings of bread are usually made to the deities, and fresh produce is a main feature of the lavish Lammas feast.

beginner's lammas ritual

The Lammas rituals include giving thanks for the harvest, honoring the mother Goddess and the first of her children (the grain harvest), as well as praising the waning Sun God as the father of the feast.

Be sure you make an offering of grain or bread to all deities, elementals, or spirits who are present.

Dancing and feasting around the balefire of the Irish sun deity, Lugh, is a prominent part of group rituals. Solitary practitioners can dance around a sturdy candle. If the candle is too dangerous or impractical, dancing around wheat or other symbols of the season is appropriate.

However you choose to honor this sabbat, be sure any energies you awaken are grounded before you consider the rites to be done.

Mabon or the Autumn Equinox (September 21 or 22)

Mabon is the name of a Welsh god who is portrayed as both child and man. This is appropriate for this time when the powers of darkness and light hang in balance before shifting their weight to the dark time of the year.

As a festival, Mabon is the name of second of the three harvest sabbats, the one usually associated with apples, berries, and other fruits from which wines and ales are made. Though our beloved deities are again growing into their elderhood, we celebrate their bounty with wine, wisdom, song, and dance.

Because the feasting at this sabbat is such an integral part of the rites, Mabon has been dubbed by some "the Witches' Thanksgiving." Others refer to it as Harvest Home, a festival popular in England until the seventeenth century.

beginner's mabon ritual

Mabon rituals include visiting cemeteries, giving apples to the ancestors by leaving them on grave stones, and drinking the wines from the previous season.

I follow a path with Celtic roots, and every Mabon I go out to my family's cemetery and offer a gift of bread or fruit to the Guardian of the Gate who watches over and protects the cemetery. Since it is considered to be sacred space by people in almost all religions, the guardian is a powerful ruler. You must always get his permission to enter and assure him you come only to honor your beloved dead.

If you are in a ritual circle, you may want to honor the Goddess and ask that her wisdom be passed down to you. You can also give thanks to Mabon, the consort of the Goddess who will give him rebirth at Yule.

As always, dismiss and ground as appropriate.

What goes around . . .

Six weeks after Mabon we're back to Samhain, and a new turn of the wheel of the year commences. Eternal and complete, all things in their own time in their own cycles. The aging Goddess contains the seed of the young God who will be reborn to her at Yule. The cycles of the seasons turn on and on.

what witches do: the esbats

The second wheel of the year is made up of the thirteen lunar cycles occurring within the solar year—called "esbats" by Pagans. Covens usually meet on either the full or the new moon and a few manage both. Solitary practitioners are urged to commemorate the moon's journey through the sky at both times, but the merrymaking and festival night has always been that of the full moon. Never forget that the word "lunatic" means "moon madness."

The great night light in the sky was humanity's first calendar. In many prepatriarchal cultures, it was considered a feminine symbol, representative of the Goddess due to the fact that its synodic, or relational, revolution around the earth takes twenty-nine days, twelve hours, and forty-four minutes, which closely matches the female menstrual cycle of twenty-eight to thirty days. Its waxing phase symbolized the virgin aspect of the Goddess, the full moon symbolized the fullness of the mother aspect, and the waning moon symbolized the aged and wise crone aspect.

In cultures which had male moon deities as well as or instead of female lunar deities, the waxing moon was the horned God of the woodlands and son of the Goddess, the full moon was the warrior and father, and the waning moon corresponded to the hunter and teacher who was the elder God.

Many cultures have assigned names to each of the thirteen full moons that usually occur within our standard solar year. The Irish have one set of names, West Africans have another set, and North Americans have created several of their own moon names, some taken from the spiritual traditions of Native Americans.

However, the fact remains that thirteen lunar months is a longer period of time than our solar year of 365 days. Thirteen full lunar cycles take approximately 374 days. Some traditions have divided their full moons into twenty-eight days, disregarding the moon's phase just so the solar and lunar years will begin and end at the same time. This occurs frequently among North American practitioners using the Irish-Celtic lunar calendar. Other Witches will simply choose to acknowledge two separate New Year's Days, or will use the Blue Moon—a second full moon falling within the same solar month—as a point to make any adjustments. For example, if the lunar months and solar months begin to diverge, they will acknowledge or ignore the Blue Moon. This keeps the Cold Moon from appearing in July, or the Harvest Moon falling in February.

For more than six thousand years, the Jewish calendar has allowed for periodic adjustments, while the Islamic lunar calendar makes none. The result being that in Islam a holy day can, and eventually will, fall within the corresponding season of the solar year.

No matter how hard we try, the two will never be an exact match, nor is there any reason they should be. In Witchcraft, we honor dual realities, why then can we not honor two separate and different, though equally important, wheels of time?

honoring the moon as we honor the sun

The moon should not occupy a lesser place in a Witch's life than the sun, and forcing the moon's thirteen cycles to match those of the sun is not only confusing, but by its very nature places the energy of the moon at the mercy of the sun.

Whatever method we choose to periodically realign the two calendars, we should never forget that the moon is as important as the sun and deserves our reverence just for being the moon. Worshiping beneath moonlight is an ancient practice, one that still motivates our primitive, atavistic centers and draws us into the moon's spell. The oldest of the sabbats is said by many to be Yule or Midwinter, with evidence of its holy placement on the solar year dating back approximately twelve thousand years. By contrast, evidence of lunar calendars dates back nearly forty thousand years.

the triple goddess

The earliest humans honored the moon as a female deity. While lunar gods and solar goddess would eventually make themselves known, the obvious connection with the menstrual cycle tended to make people think of womanhood.

The three phases of the moon spoke to our ancestors of the cycles of death, renewal, and rebirth. Over the course of twenty-nine days, the moon seemed to mimick the familiar cycle of death and rebirth. Since birth was a feminine function, the moon became female.

The deity as a three-in-one god did not originate in Christianity. The moon's three phases were also correlated with the three phases of a woman's life: virgin, mother, and crone. The moon embodied these three faces and gave rise to the worship of these three-in-one deities.

During the waxing phase, we have our virgin Goddess, adventurous, sexual, able to traverse all worlds that open to her beauty and prowess. At the full phase, we have the nurturing mother, powerful, protective, and strong. In the waning phase, we have the crone, the elder grandmother moon with her wit, wisdom, and no-nonsense ways.

We honor all these aspects through our rituals and we can and do draw on each of these phases to assist us in magick—as we'll see later.

exploring the hidden self

If you've read the astrological profiles for your sun sign and noticed things that didn't ring true for you, then you're probably only seeing a small portion of your personality represented. Every planet in our solar system and every aspect between them tells part of the picture that makes each of us unique.

The sun's placement in your horoscope is what you say when someone asks, "What's your sign?" The sun is our outer self, the side we show to the world whether it feels right to do so or not. The moon's placement in your natal chart, on the other hand, tells you about your inner self, the part you keep hidden, sometimes even from yourself.

I struggled with this as a teenager. My sun sign is Leo, but deep inside I didn't feel like the archetypical Leo, even though my parents saw me as one. And if they saw me this way, it's likely the rest of the world viewed me as a Leo personality. Inside, I hid strong empathic impulses, a tendency to be discontent, and I was drawn to all forms of divination. These are some of the traits of a person with a moon in Pisces. Once I had the whole picture, I was able to make more sense of why I was who I was.

You can find the placement of your moon in an ephemeris, which can be found in many books on astrology. I've included brief descriptions of lunar characteristics in appendix 2. Take a close look at the inner you and see if it doesn't complete the puzzle of your personality as much as it did for me. If you don't know where your moon falls in the zodiac, try to see if you can guess which one you are by reading through the descriptions.

the esbat celebration

Many Witches who practice their faith alone will take advantage of both the new and full moons to celebrate, and will call both of these events an esbat. Due to the many demands on everyone's time, covens and other groups will usually choose one or the other, with the full moon being the most popular.

The word *esbat* (pronounced ESS-bott) is derived from the same root as the word *estrus*, a Greek word meaning "of the month," for the fertile heat periods of female mammals.

The dark, new moon esbat is a chance to worship the darker aspects of the Craft. This is not be confused with evil or negative aspects. The dark is simply that which is hidden, that which is in shadow rather than in light, and closely reflects our inner lives in the same way the sun reflects our light outer selves.

The full moon esbat tends to be a ribald, frenetic celebration—suitable for the "lunatics" who were once believed to display their insanity under the light of the full moon.

Magick for all manner of needs is enacted during esbat rituals, both in group settings and by solitary practitioners.

Spells for increase or gain are usually done during the waxing phases, and spells for decrease or loss are performed during the waning period. The full moon is used for spells for wholeness, children and mothers, families, psychic enhancement, and some love spells.

The two major components of any full-moon esbat are two rituals that you must become familiar with if you want to call yourself a Witch. These are Drawing Down the Moon and the Ceremony of Cakes and Ale.

Drawing Down the Moon

Until you have some experience channeling outside energies, you will probably be only a witness to this powerful ritual of invocation. Even so, the experience can be a profound one, if you can observe a coven that is able to enact this ritual with ease.

The idea behind it is to draw the essence of the Moon Mother, or lunar Goddess, into the body of a coven member. The person chosen is usually a priestess or leader, but this is not always the case. Even men may have the lunar Goddess—or God, if you prefer—occupy their physical bodies. You'll find lots of experiments with androgyny in Pagan ritual the deeper into it you go.

Drawing Down the Moon can also be enacted by a solitary practitioner, but the ceremony has more meaning and, well, just more grandeur, when performed by a group outdoors under the moon's fullest light. Through the body of the priestess, the Goddess speaks to us. She may answer questions or give instructions. She may offer someone who needs some extra attention or a special blessing from her. Or she may just pour her loving energy into the circle and lead you in a merry spiral dance.

How do we know that this is the Goddess leading us and that this is not some play-acting done to heighten the ego of a priestess? When you start working with energies outside yourself, when you learn to draw from and channel them, you become an expert on sensing what is sacred and what is Witchcrap. Any priestess faking the Goddess within would be quickly unmasked, and most would never resort to trying such a game.

The transfer of Goddess to Witch is made by having another person experienced in drawing and channeling energies pull down the lunar energy. If the person into whom the Goddess will be drawn is a woman, then a man is usually chosen to do the drawing. Likewise, if the energy is to be channeled into a man, a woman is likely to be the one who will draw down the energy. There is no law that says it must be this way, but it's always best to keep everything balanced, and that includes the potent polarity of male and female energies.

The priest doing the drawing down of the moon may choose a chalice, usually of silver, or a double-sided ritual knife, known as an athame (pronounced ah-THAW-may or ATH-um-may), as a receptacle for the lunar energy he wishes to transfer into the body of the priestess. He and the priestess will stand face to face in the center of the circle, in a position where the priest can see the full moon directly over the head of the priestess. He will raise the chalice or blade to a point where, from his perspective, the tool touches the moon's face. He then leads the coven in an invocation asking the Moon Goddess to use the tool as a catalyst for coming down into the body of her priestess. When the priest feels the divine energy entering the tool, he brings it down and touches it to either forehead, heart center, or womb area of the priestess until she feels the Goddess has entered her body. As he draws in the moon, he may wish to seal his efforts by making an invoking pentagram sign in the air in front of the priestess (see illustration below).

Pentagram Signs

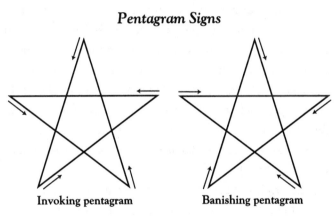

Invoking pentagram   Banishing pentagram

There's no mistaking this transformation. Everyone in the circle will feel the shift in energies and, in some cases, the priestess will even look and sound like a different person.

When the ritual is complete, the priest reverses the invoking process and returns the lunar energy to the moon.

When the energy is returned, the priest may make the sign of the banishing, or dismissal, pentagram in front of the priestess (see illustration on previous page), and then stay near to her as she reorients herself to the circle atmosphere again.

Cakes and Ale

The Ceremony of Cakes and Ale is an easy ritual to perform, and one that is very common at esbats. It usually concludes any esbat ritual whether it is a group or a solitary affair. In fact, it's one you can do yourself if you want to start practicing the Craft on the very next full moon.

The format and concept may already be familiar to you. If you grew up as a Christian, you will notice the similarity between the Pagan ritual and the Christian communion service, which sees the bread and wine as symbolic of the body and blood of their savior deity, Jesus. If you grew up Jewish, you will notice the similarity to the *Kiddush*, or wine blessing, and the *Hamotzi*, or the thanking of God for the gift of bread.

The origins of breaking bread with another person as a sign of connection and goodwill go deep into prehistory, when bread and wine were staples of the small tribes of humans who had ceased their nomadic ways. Bread could be had all year long if the grain harvest was properly preserved, and fermented liquids bypassed the dangers of diseases that were carried in tainted water supplies.

For this ritual, you will need a small portion of bread and some type of drink in a cup or chalice. Do not feel you have to use an alcoholic beverage. Many covens substitute juice or even water out of concern for others who may be in recovery. Use what feels best to you. I often use plain water into which I've placed some lemon, a fruit sometimes associated with lunar energies.

"Cake" is also another word that is flexible and can be misleading, since most covens use cookies or loaves of bread for this ritual.

Bread and wine symbolize the body of the great Mother Goddess and the blood of her womb from which all things are born. This is why the Goddess is associated with the esbat celebration; regardless of how many lunar Gods exist, Wicca tends to view the full moon as a feminine symbol ruled by a feminine deity.

Whatever the deity, place the bread and drink onto some type of central altar. Take the bread first and hold it before you as if you were offering it to someone else. Speak words of blessing that focus on the gift of the bread from the Goddess rather than blessing the bread itself. Something like:

> Blessed be the Goddess who gives herself to us
> in the form of a bountiful harvest. Blessed be
> her bread, the gift of her body that sustains
> and nurtures us. By all that is sacred, so mote
> it be.

Break off a small piece of the bread and eat it. If there are others working with you, pass the bread clockwise around your circle. Each person should break off a piece of the bread and eat it. As each person sends the loaf on around the circle, you may feel free to offer a blessing to that person, such as, "I pass the gift of life to you," or "Here is the Goddess to feed the Goddess within."

Next you will take up the chalice and hold it up, also as if offering it someone else. The blessing will be similar to that said over the bread:

> Blessed be the womb of the Goddess in whose
> blood we are formed and from which we are
> born. Blessed be her gift of drink which links us
> to her powers of creation. From her womb we
> came, and to it we shall one day return to await
> rebirth. By all that is sacred, so mote it be.

Take a drink from the chalice and, if you are working with others, pass the chalice clockwise around the circle so everyone may drink or honor the blood of the Goddess in their own way. No one should be forced to drink. Some people have allergies to certain juices or to the sulfites in wines, and others may be in recovery. Some fear getting or passing illnesses. Those who wish not to consume the drink may bow to the chalice, hold it to the heart or fore-head, or raise it in a toast to the moon.

As with the bread, you may feel free to give a blessing to the person to whom you pass the chalice. This might be something like: "I give you the gift of life, the blood of the

Goddess, our mother" or, "Herein is the blood of the Goddess who blesses us with life renewed."

When your ritual is complete, you should take the chalice and remaining bread outdoors. Pour any liquid onto the ground and place the leftover bread on top of it. The liquid is a libation, your offering to the Goddess of the earth, and the bread is a sacrifice that her animals can enjoy. You may even want to make a statement out loud as you give these offerings. A simple sentence telling the Goddess what you're giving her and thanking her is sufficient, but you may be as elaborate as you like.

Last of all, be sure to ground yourself when you are finished with this or any other ritual.

"are you a good witch, or a bad witch?"

How many times have we heard the fluttery voice of actress Billie Burke, dressed up like a huge, pink birthday cake, address this question to the confused Dorothy Gale, who just rode into Munchkinland from Kansas on the last tornado? Probably more times than we can count. Witch Glinda expected a black or white answer. In modern Wicca, the terms "good" and "bad" are not at all black and white. As you may have guessed from your reading so far, it just isn't that simple.

We first need to talk about how modern Witchcraft treats the terms "black magick" and "white magick," how and why we determine who is a good Witch or a bad Witch, and when it's none of our business to know or to interfere. Even the most experienced of Witches must go back to the beginning and assess a situation in terms of "As it harms none."

is "harm none" a realistic goal?

Some Witches debate whether it's realistic to believe that any deliberate change in the energy fields surrounding us can really harm none. I tend to disagree with this assessment for two reasons. First of all, the universe is full of abundance, so that no one has to lose out so that someone else can have things. Secondly, change that affects someone occurs all the time. Even doing nothing can have repercussions. Better to choose your path of action than to allow things to just happen.

For example, take that stop sign at your local intersection. It was erected to change the flow of traffic, presumably so that no one will be harmed, yet if it slows you down getting to work, then you might see it as harm done. In truth the harm-none and greater-good ideals were served by the stop sign. Next time, leave earlier.

Repercussions are real, though, and they are the reasons you won't find many Witches engaging in magick without first doing divinations—such as reading tarot cards or casting rune stones—to get a peek at the outcome of a spell before they enact it. This requires that the entire spell be planned out ahead of time—words, gestures, visualizations, tools, etc.—so that the divination can take all these elements, combine them, and give you an accurate reading based on all the known factors that are in motion at the time of the divination.

Change even one word of the spell or how you visualize it, and you send another chain of cause and effect out onto the wheel of existence, where it will pick up many hitch-hikers before returning to you. This means doing divination before enacting the spell is not optional; it's necessary, and it's the responsible thing to do (and we'll cover the basics of divination the next chapter).

shades of gray

Many modern Witches shun the terms "white magick" and "black magick," and I agree with their decision. Nothing we do in the Craft is so clear-cut that we can attach to it such extreme labels. Along the spell continuum are many shades of gray, including that murky gray line that tips your magick from positive to negative without anyone realizing it's occurred until it's too late to put on the brakes.

We've already established that Witchcraft is the spiritual pathway for the responsible. If you chose to engage in manipulative actions, then you must remember that only you will reap the sorrow they will bring. Stepping outside the bounds of a religious framework will not excuse you from this threefold karma. If you believe in the ever-turning wheel of existence that makes our magick work, then you have to accept also that that same wheel brings back to us our own intent and the intent of everyone else. Either the wheel turns or it doesn't. You'll find you cannot embrace it when it's convenient and cast it aside when its not.

This cycle of cause and effect is one reason why the terms "black magick" and "white magick" are not heard within the Craft. They simply make no sense in our worldview. A simple reading of world mythology shows that the Pagan deities are not wholly good or evil; they just are. Some give in to petty jealousies, some kill, some heal, some love us like a parent, and some are tricksters willing to have a laugh at our expense. There are no deities who can be tossed with ease into the black camp or the white camp. We were created in their images—God and Goddess, male and female—and, like our deities, no witch is perfect. We all just do the best we can with what we have.

being a good witch

Being a good Witch does not make you perfect. If our deities are not infallible, then how can we be, for we are of their images? Being a good Witch means doing your best for self and all other beings, both the seen and unseen. It means living in harmony with nature, whether your nature is in a cottage in a forest or a big city highrise.

Above all else, being a good Witch means that you can be trusted—by yourself, others, and the deities—to make the most ethical choices you can based on the information you have available. And if you do unintentionally cause harm, you're willing to correct the problem, even if doing so means you don't get what you wanted in the end.

Too many people come to Wicca because of the omnipotent power they think they will possess once they learn our secret handshake. It just doesn't work that way. Magick can make you feel powerful; that is true, but it is also humbling to have the power of creation like your deities. Only the self-responsible can use that power without getting burned in the end. Ask around and you'll find Witches who can tell you some real horror stories of their first magickal efforts and how dearly they paid for not heeding the warning of the Rede.

black and white as magickal colors

The words "black" and "white," as they are used by Witches today, do not refer to positive or negative values or to ethics but rather to the properties of these two colors as they apply to magic. We all know, for instance, that black can be warm to the touch. This is especially true if black fabric has been left outside under the sun. This is because black color is the result of all light being absorbed by a surface. Black holds inside itself all light energy, therefore it is often employed in spells where you want something to be absorbed or collected so it can be used or disposed of.

By contrast, white reflects all colors of the light spectrum equally. This is why white fabrics remain cool to the touch and are often used in lightweight clothing for summer. Because it covers all contingencies, white is always an appropriate magickal substitute when you aren't sure what color candle, ink, stone, etc. is best for any particular ritual or spell. You can never go wrong with white.

green magick

The only color magick you will hear about from most Wiccans is green magick, also known as eco-magick. This is magick done for and within the natural environment. Creating a garden full of magickal herbs is green magick. Cultivating healing plants is green magick. Enacting spells to heal an ailing tree or to protect endangered animals and plants is green magick.

Because Witchcraft is a nature or earth religion, in some way, we all practice green magick. We view the earth as the body of the great Mother Goddess, and we do whatever we can to honor and cherish her.

the basics of divination

Divination and magick are linked in the same way branches of government are connected. They each have their own spheres of influence, they support and correct our magickal course, and they act as a system of checks and balances on each other.

"Divination" comes from the Greek *divinos*, meaning "something that comes from the deities." In ancient Greek myth, the deities were expected to have all the answers and to solve everyone's problems.

For us, divination is simply a method by which we read future outcomes of proposed thoughts and actions already set in motion. Divination doesn't read the future as a certainty but as it stands now, with all the current influences upon it that create the potential of a specific outcome. We are never at the mercy of the Fates. If we were, there would be no point in bothering with divinations. We are always in control. By changing our current course, we can change the outcome.

Divination can be done by reading tarot cards, casting wands or stones, reading patterns in nature, seeking omens in birds (often called augury rather than divination), or scrying (gazing into a reflective surface such as a crystal or pool of water).

As I've already said, divination and magick go hand in hand in Witchcraft. We don't do magick without first doing a divination. A divination is always performed after all elements of a spell have been created. Just by conceptualizing how your spell will be enacted, your mind is already imprinting its will on the wheel of existence, and you need to make sure that it won't hurt anyone during its rotation or hurt you when it comes back.

how divination works

We are all connected within the web of existence, and all time and space is wherever we are now. We may perceive our lives as separate and moving along on a linear course, but both physics and metaphysics will tell you otherwise.

When we are all connected, all we have to do is reach out to collect information from anyone, in any place, and from any time.

Twentieth-century psychologist Carl Jung referred to this great source of knowledge as the "collective unconscious." He imagined our combined mindsets and assumptions about the ways thing are, were, or will be as a huge open book in which anything we could ever want to know has been recorded and can be tapped into by us.

If you're working with a long-term issue or a question that is in a state of flux, divination will read only potentials currently set into motion. Something someone is only thinking about doing will impact a little on the divination. An action someone has taken will affect it more. An action that someone is determined to take will show up in the divination.

It's this latter concept that's hardest to work with, and why it is sometimes not a good idea to rush into an action for a spell without doing several divinations and watching how the potential outcomes change with your changing intent.

Whatever you do, keep close records in your Book of Shadows so you'll know for the future what a particular card or item means for you.

divination methods

Most Witches have a favorite form of divination. Runes, ancient Nordic or Teutonic glyphs carved into flat polished stones, are a favorite among those following Nordic or Teutonic traditions. Lots or wands are popular among Celtic and Middle Eastern traditions, and a majority of Witches have at least one tarot card deck they like.

If you don't already practice a particular divination technique, a good way to get started is with scrying and tarot. While you are searching for and becoming accustomed to a deck of tarot cards, you can begin to work on scrying. This will allow you to start training your mind in the divinatory arts without having you make a major investment of money. All this will take from you is some time and energy.

Choosing a tarot deck

I love the rich symbolism of the tarot cards and collect decks I have no intention of using for divination just because I'm enamored of the artwork. The one I use for divination is *The Robin Wood Tarot* (Llewellyn Publications), for its Pagan imagery and lush artistry. Before it was published I used the popular *Rider-Waite Tarot* (published by U.S. Games).

Take your time selecting the deck you feel will work best for you. Most occult shops and many large bookstores will either keep a deck accessible so you can examine the art before you buy or have representative cards behind a glass display counter.

Sealed decks for which there are no examples might have unsealed companion books or booklets that will have pictures of the cards, sometimes in black and white, but these will give you some idea of how you feel about the overall concept of the cards.

You will not often be allowed to randomly look through decks because the vendors want to keep the energies of the deck as undisturbed as possible. After you purchase a deck you like, you will need to spend a lot of time shuffling the cards, meditating on them, studying their imagery, and comparing your intuitive sense of the cards with the artist's concept, which is usually found in a small instruction book inside the deck's box. You'll want to handle them as much as you can. Breathe on them. Sleep with them. They won't work their best unless they are attuned to you and your personal vibrations.

Record your feelings about specific cards in your Book of Shadows. Even more important, once you start trying to read the cards (instructions are provided inside the deck's box and there are a great many good books on tarot divination for beginners) be sure that you date and record the question or issue you asked about, and note which cards appeared. What is not clear today may make perfect sense in another week or two.

Scrying 101

While you're making your search for a suitable tarot deck, you can explore your psychic skills via a divination method known as scrying. Scrying requires no expensive equipment. You probably have a suitable scrying surface in or near your house. Scrying is merely the art of gazing into a mirror, a crystal, a pool of liquid, or a flame until mental impression—or even full-blown, movie-scene-type images—of an outcome appear to you. Scrying is what happens when someone gazes into the clichéd crystal ball.

The trick to scrying success is not to work very hard at it. Famous turn-of-the-century ceremonial magician Aleister Crowley referred to this state of mind as your "will-less will." In other words, you're working hard to make your magick work, but you're also very casual about what you're doing, and you're detached from the outcome.

If the question is about an issue dear to you, this can be a difficult state of mind to achieve. To help with this, think of the nonchalance of a big cat who appears to be more interested in grooming a paw than in chasing some nearby prey. You'd never know what was on that cat's mind if it didn't leap up all of a sudden to make a graceful and successful grab at its quarry. That's the power of your will-less will.

As you gaze at your chosen object, try to look into it rather than at it or past it. Keep your mind focused solely on the issue at hand. This may be a question about possible adverse outcomes of a spell you want to do. You may be scrying to gain information for yourself, asking the deities for something you need to learn right now. You can also get answers to a problem or divine the future for yourself or anyone else.

If your mind starts to wander—and it will at first, just as it did when you first started to learn meditation—just bring it back where you want it to be. Don't let the mental wandering upset you. This is all part of your training. If you become fidgety or tense, you will lose the "will-less will" sensation, and be back to the beginning again.

Some people find they have an affinity for scrying and get very good results right from the start. Others find it more difficult. Only practice will get you into that state of receptive mind that's ready to accept impressions or view scenarios.

the physics of magick

Modern Witches don't have to defend magick as a science any longer. Well, let's say we don't have to champion its validity as vigorously as we once did. Over time, science has proven many concepts about time and space that Witches have accepted for centuries. Case in point: the theory that time is not linear.

Before you take your first step into magick, you have to discard one word from your vocabulary: "supernatural." Expunge it from your mind. Apply it to nothing, to no one, and to no event. The reason?

Nothing supernatural can exist.

We may not understand all the natural laws under which the universe operates, but all things, living and nonliving, are governed by them. We may not understand these laws at this precise moment, but we know they must exist. A cat will not grow wings, winter will not follow spring, immortality cannot be reached via alchemy, a tree cannot be a maple one summer and become a sycamore the next, and gravity will always hold us in its grip. All of these are natural laws of science or, if you prefer, of our creator or creators. Logically, these natural laws must include the laws governing magickal operations. Everything in the known universe operates under a set of natural laws because it cannot do otherwise. We can harness the energies around us for temporary use, but we cannot change their character or the laws under which they operate.

If you must use a term for something you don't understand, but which continues to happen anyway, refer to it as "paranormal." This word refers to a function outside the boundaries of what we think of as a natural occurrence, while still acknowledging that the occurrence is wholly natural, because it has to be. We can be sure that, somewhere, a natural law is at work governing the paranormal event.

Magick is simply the art of using energies not yet fully understood by science but which can still be used to cause physical reality to change in accordance with one's magickal will. I envision that magickal results are accomplished using that same wheel of existence we discussed when we were examining magickal ethics. What we send out on the wheel is affected not only by our will but by the wills of millions of other people and by discarnates and nonhumans with strong personalities. When the magickal energy returns, it has attracted to itself similar energies. In other words, positive will give positive results. Negative will attracts negative results.

Thus we learn a natural law: like energies attract like energies. This is why we meditate, bathe, and clear our minds before entering sacred space or enacting magick or ritual. We want to attract only the highest, brightest, and best to work with us. In his book *The Golden Bough*, Sir James Frazer called this kind of magick "sympathetic magic."

Another magickal analogy uses the four elements (earth, air, fire, and water) plus the element of spirit as a model. We live our normal lives just below the vibratory arena of the element of earth, while the thoughts that first coalesce into our magickal will are living in a realm just above the element of spirit. As we continue to feed energy into our desire, the mental picture of what we want solidifies and that weight drags it down through the lighter elements of air and fire. Then it spirals down toward us through water and earth, all the while attracting to it positive or negative qualities, until it is too dense for the elemental realms, and your magickal will manifests in the physical world.

avoiding consequences

Some try to mentally divorce themselves from the Craft, thinking this will allow them to escape the Threefold Law. Remember those natural laws of the universe? They remain in place. So, can you bypass the karmic retributions of negative magick by placing yourself outside of a spiritual practice or religion, including Wicca?

Absolutely not.

If you believe in the mechanism that makes magick work, then you must also accept that that same mechanism brings back energies other than your own. You are not the only being with a will living in the universe, therefore you cannot claim your own personal wheel of existence. The mechanism is there for all to use. Accept the responsibility or don't use it. What you can't do is make a universal action your own private magick machine. Like will attract like, no matter who you are. You either believe in and accept that this is how energy operates, or you don't. There's no picking and choosing when or if you want it there or not. If you deny the wheel, than you deny yourself magickal goals. If the wheel could not bring retribution for your negative actions, it also could not bring you your magickal desires.

six prerequisites for successful spellcraft

Witches often hone these six prerequisites for successful spellwork into a four-part phrase that reads:

> To know, to will, to dare, to keep silent.

I add two others that I believe round out the formula and give the novice magician a better grasp of the background necessary for providing the best environment for your spells to thrive.

1. Desire and need

2. Emotional involvement

3. Knowledge and realistic expectations

4. Belief

5. The ability to keep silent

6. Willingness to back up magick in the physical world

Desire and need

Desire and need are the impulses that drive the Witch to construct a plausible spell to enact a positive change. You have to have a need that feeds your desire for change, and you have to desire the change enough that it's a real need. Only when you cannot mentally separate the desire from the need are you ready to use them as the beginning magickal catalyst. This creates links to the wished for outcome both on the physical and otherworldly planes, where spells must first take shape before they can be drawn into physical manifestation.

When desire and need become one in your mind, you will then develop the second requirement—emotional involvement.

Emotional involvement

Your emotional involvement is fueled by your desire and need, and your desire and need help you forge the emotional link to your goal that enhances the magickal energies you propose to bring forth. Emotional involvement does this by creating a personal investment in the outcome intense enough to allow you to see the spell through to its end. Whether it's good for your or not, anything to which you have an emotional attachment, or investment in, is very hard to let go.

The least effective spells are ones you ask someone else to do for you. Chances are someone else will not do a good job for you, even if that person is a skilled Witch, because the necessary emotional involvement just isn't going to be there. Emotional attachment to your goal is like putting gas in your car; it's the go-juice that sets things into motion.

No matter how deep your emotions run, magick does you no good if it flies in the face of the natural laws of the universe or if you have no means or knowledge to enact it.

Knowledge and realistic expectations

You must have enough magickal knowledge to be able to construct an appropriate spell. By appropriate I mean one in which the expectations for the outcome are not only ethical, but plausible. I'll repeat what I've written a dozen times before: magick will not make you fly, but it can get you good seats on a safe plane or help you to astral project.

Magick will not make some glamorous celebrity whom you've never met fall madly in love with you, though it can help you meet this person or find love closer to home. Magick will not make you rich, but it can help you find prosperity in places you might never have thought to look.

Knowledge about magickal operations will come to you in time, and it will be an ongoing quest in your Craft career. Sooner than you realize, you'll know how to select the best day of the week or phase of the moon in which to cast your spell, and your idea of reality and plausible outcomes will expand.

With knowledge comes self-confidence, and this in turns creates confidence in your efforts.

Belief

It has often been said that each mind is a universe unto itself. What your mind believes becomes your reality. Believing that you spell will work requires you to expand your thinking to view the full 360-degree circle of your world. This is something that usually doesn't happen until you gain some practical experience through meditation or astral projection, two arts that impress upon us the cyclic and omnipresent nature of creation. For the best outcomes, you must believe in yourself and your power to make positive changes in your life.

You may need to keep believing even when things seem to be going wrong. You may even need to reenact the spell. You also need to keep all this effort to yourself.

Keeping silent

Keeping silent about your magick protects both the spell and the energy you've put into it. People's jealousies can manifest as thoughtforms that can affect your magick. Even your best friend may resent your seeking something she does not have. This person may not even realize she doesn't want you to achieve your goals, perhaps from fear of being left behind in your life.

Talking about your magick weakens its connection to your own energy field by dissipating it. The more you talk about your spell, the more energy you siphon off from it, until it's too weak to work for you. Put your energy into strengthening your magickal will and not into chatter about personal goals that are best kept to yourself.

In your silence, you must actively seek to manifest your will in any way you can.

Backing up magick in the physical world

Magick is not a panacea for all woes. It won't work for you if you're not out helping it along. For example, if you want a new house, you have to apply for loans and go out seeking your dream home. Magick can help you obtain both, but you still have to do the legwork yourself. Magick can also help you find the love of your life, but you have to get out where you have a reasonable chance of meeting this person. Prince Charming or Princess Enchantra will not come knocking at your door otherwise.

Even Judeo-Christian traditions teach that "God helps those who help themselves." If you really want something, then prove it to the deities by making it a daily goal.

the six magickal skills

There are many different magickal skills, and if you stick with Witchcraft, you'll learn many more of them. The six listed below are the building blocks that everyone must first develop to perform even the most simple operation. Once you get a good grasp on these six, there's virtually no spell or ritual you cannot enact successfully.

Don't worry at this stage in your Witchcraft studies about mastering these. Begin to work with them one at a time, doing your best to perform them longer, stronger, and clearer each time you try. For the first year and a day of your studies, you will work to get better at each of these. This will not only make your magick stronger, but it will enhance your meditation, dream recall, and energy manipulation skills.

Remember, these six skills may at first appear simple, but they are the foundation of all magickal success. The six basic magickal skills are:

1. Visualization

2. Centering and balancing

3. Raising and sending magickal energy

4. Charging, enchanting, and empowering

5. Altering consciousness

6. Grounding excess energy

In theory all of these are simple skills, so much so that we might be given to wonder why everyone is not using them to work magickal miracles in their lives every day. The truth is that, though they are easy to conceptualize, they can be hard to master if the student refuses to practice or chooses to fool himself about his abilities. It takes time to learn how to hold all these processes in your mind and still focus on your magickal intent. When looked at from that perspective, magick may seem overwhelming now, but you'll be surprised at how it starts to come naturally as you practice the skills daily.

Please, for the sake of your Craft, commit to the daily practice of these skills. It's only through practice that you gain knowledge, and it's only by knowledge that you attain spiritual wisdom and magickal success.

Skill #1: Visualization

Visualization is the single most important magickal skill you will learn, yet it seems to be the most misunderstood. I receive many letters and e-mails from novices and initiates alike who claim they cannot visualize.

That's just not possible. If you're alive you can think, and if you can think you can visualize. When you read, don't pictures appear in your mind? When someone tells you about their wonderful vacation, don't pictures of how it must have been pop into your head? Any mental picture that you hold on to is a visualization. Your meditation skills will help you do this. As with meditation, if your mind wanders, bring it back where you want it until it knows who's in charge.

Always visualize your goal as complete, as if it were a done deal in your life. Visualizing or wording any magick in the future tense keep your magick in the future, forever just out of your reach.

Thought must always precede action regardless of which world the thought is in. All the greatest inventions in the world began life as a spark of idea in someone's mind. That someone molded and fleshed out an idea with visualization, then took physical-world action to make the visualization come into reality.

When you focus on a single scene or on a whole mental movie, you are feeding it energy. As your junior-high science teacher taught you, matter cannot be created or destroyed, it may only change forms. With visualization you are working to transform energies already around and within you. Eventually the mental image is so real that it gains in density and must leave the astral, or unseen, realm and come into our physical world. We may also enter that unseen or astral realm by learning to send our consciousness out into other worlds and times. We call this process astral projection, an art which can be learned. Look on the Internet or in bookstores for detailed instructions on this practice.

If you're still having trouble, or think you are, try working with these two visualization-enhancing exercises.

visualization exercise 1

Find yourself a quiet, private place, and get comfortable. You may lie down if you're not afraid of falling asleep. Don't cross your legs or put pressure on areas of your body that will become sore or fall asleep from lack of bloodflow. This will only make staying in your altered mental state more difficult.

Once you've relaxed, I want you to envision a room with which you are familiar. Allow a mental picture of the room to fall into place. Once it does, expand on the details by recalling what art is on the walls, what color wallpaper or paint it has, how many pieces of furniture there are, and note the placement of any books or magazines that are usually left lying around.

Do this every day until you suddenly find the details popping into their correct places all on their own. You are seeing with your mind, therefore you are visualizing.

visualization exercise 2

Again you will need that quiet, private place in which to work undisturbed. Once you are comfortable and relaxed, envision that same room, again in full detail.

Now play with making changes. Imagine a specific knickknack disappearing and reappearing elsewhere in the room. Also envision new items coming in from other rooms. These items may pop quickly in and out, or they may fade in and out, whatever feels best to you.

As you play this mind game, you may notice that someone else in your home feels compelled to move the item you're working with in accordance with your mental picture. This is magick in action. Your reality is conforming to your will.

Both of these exercises are useful in helping you build your astral projection skills, too—ones you will use later on when you gain more control over all three levels of your mind: the subconscious, the conscious, and the superconscious.

Skill #2: Centering and balancing

Centering and balancing are often synonymous, but there are subtle differences. Balancing means that you have all your power centers open and fully functioning so that you are a perfect conduit for the magickal energy you will be drawing in. It also means that you feel at peace and you've released all earthly problems and negative energies before you open your sacred space or start to do any spell or ritual. You must balance before you can center. To balance yourself means to be in harmony with the energies of the universe. It also means to have all those energies equally distributed in yourself.

Centering means drawing your consciousness deep into yourself to fuel your center of power. You do this by envisioning energy coming from high up above you in the heavenly realms or from deep below you in Mother Earth. This prevents you from using up your own power and petering out before you can complete your magick.

the tree meditation

A common and popular exercise for balancing and centering is to stand up and imagine yourself as the trunk of a huge tree. The World Tree meditation on page 54 is a good example.

chakras

Another way to balance and center is to mentally cleanse, energize, and open your chakra centers. *Chakra* is a Sanskrit word meaning "wheel," and it refers to the seven major energy centers that are aligned down the human body from top of the head to tailbone. These energy centers were discovered in India hundreds of years ago and have been used by Witches ever since to provide balance and to raise and project power. The major chakras are illustrated in the drawing on the facing page and in the table below.

Chakra Name	Location	Color
Crown chakra	On top of the head	Violet
Brow chakra	Just above the eyes	Indigo
Throat chakra	Near the larynx	Blue
Heart chakra	Center of breastbone	Green
Solar plexus chakra	Beneath breastbone	Yellow
Navel chakra	Just below the navel	Orange
Root chakra	Base of the tailbone	Red

Major Chakra Points

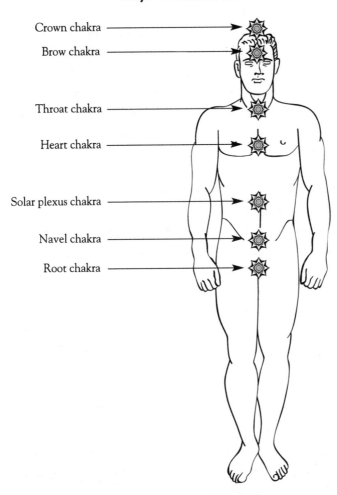

Crown chakra

Brow chakra

Throat chakra

Heart chakra

Solar plexus chakra

Navel chakra

Root chakra

There are also lesser chakra points in the palms of your hands, the soles of your feet, at the base of your neck, in the small of your back, and just above the inside of your knees.

Envision each of the major seven chakras as a bright, clear globes of spiritual light firing off and collecting a balanced and harmonic energy as you work with them. This is another exercise that you will build on in the future to work magick.

Skill #3: Raising and sending magickal energy

Remember that one of the ways we defined "Witch" is "a bender and shaper of energy"? The energy you draw on is your magickal power. When you feel you've absorbed as much as you can, you send it out to do your will. This is usually accomplished by visualizing it going to a person, place, or object, or into your mental vision.

Some new Witches are afraid of expending too much energy for fear of hurting themselves. This cannot happen if you have drawn and expanded your personal energy reserves through visualization. Dancing, drumming, and singing can also help stir the energies as well as help them go on toward your will. When you're done, you will feel similar to the way you feel after a good workout. You're a bit spent, but mostly you feel good about yourself, as if you've just recharged your low battery. To send out your raised energy, center the power you have raised within yourself by directing it to a single location within yourself. The brow, heart, or solar plexus chakra centers are the ones usually selected. But your arms are also useful. As you visualize the energy being sent out, you should mentally reinforce your mental projection by making a gesture like tossing, lifting, exhaling, or any other movement that signals to your mind that energy is being sent.

Skill #4: Charging, enchanting, and empowering

These three words are synonymous in magick. They refer to sending personal energy into an object that will act as a catalyst for magick. Popular catalysts are herbs, stones, or other talismans known to possess energy in harmony with your goal. For example, roses are associated with romantic love, cinnamon with protection, obsidian with banishing, or pentacles with harmony.

The magickal power is always within the Witch making the magick, but catalysts help us attune that power to our goals. To empower a catalyst, take the object and hold it firmly in your power, or projective, hand. (This is the hand that is dominant for you. In other words, if you say you are right-handed, your right hand is your power hand.) You can also send empowerment into an object by sending energy into it through your hands, or, similarly, you can employ any one of the chakra points to aid you.

For best results, spend as much time as you can holding and fondling the object, allowing your own energies to merge with the object before proceeding with the spell.

Skill #5: Altering consciousness

Achieving an altered state of consciousness is a study unto itself. When the cycles per second of your brain waves slow down, your mind goes into a receptive state. This makes your thoughts accessible to all worlds, and it places your mind in the perfect frame for magick. In this altered state, all visualization has magickal potential. Practice the exercises from chapter 4 to gain skill in this area. The table below shows brain wave levels in various states of consciousness.

State	Cycles per second	Condition
Beta	13–18	Normal wakefulness, alertness, conversational level. (Person is aware of all physical sensations and bodily needs.)
Alpha	7–13	Light to medium meditation, daydreaming, focused concentration, very light sleep. (Person finds waking from this level not difficult.)
Theta	4–7	Deep meditation, medium to deep sleep, light unconsciousness. (Person finds waking from this level moderately to very difficult.)
Delta	0.5–4	Very deep sleep, coma, or deep unconsciousness. (Person has little or no consciousness of physical sensations or bodily needs.)

Human beings cannot avoid falling in and out of altered states of consciousness. We are altered when we read, daydream, or watch television. If our brain waves didn't slow down, we would be unable to concentrate or sleep. We must keep in mind that these times are full of magickal potential, but we need never fear them. Here are a few techniques to help lower your brain into an alpha state:

- Mentally focus on one object or phrase.

- Count backwards from one hundred.

- Visualize yourself falling through endless space.

- Count your exhalations.

- Focus on the center of your mind, seeing it as the seat of your will.

- Recite in your mind or out loud a mantra or phrase which has meaning to you; a simple word or affirmation is sufficient.

- Gaze into a candle flame or dark bowl of water until your eyes become heavy and your mind slows.

- Take deep rhythmic breaths, counting several beats for the inhalation and the same for the exhalation.

- Visualize your mind as a blank screen and attempt to think of nothing at all.

- Sit completely still and focus on the rhythm of your heartbeats; they will slow as your brain waves slow.

Skill #6 Grounding excess energy

You may be tired of hearing this by now, but you *must* ground yourself of excess energy once any psychic exercise has been performed. Get into the habit now so that when you are capable of greater feats of magick, you won't also have to deal with greater astral nasties coming after you because they're attracted to your residual ritual energy.

putting it all together

Those are the six skills you need to practice each day. Start with visualization and work on it for one full week, being sure to add the grounding after each session. After a week has passed, add the centering and balancing work.

Go down the list this way each week until you're working with all six skills, grounding after each one.

when not to practice magickal skills

Properly enacted, magick will not seriously deplete your personal energy stores, but it does require effort, and that in itself can sometimes be tiring. Just as you wouldn't go out and run a marathon if you were stressed or sick, you shouldn't overtax an already overexerted system with magickal efforts. Even though most of the activity seems to be taking place in your head, your whole body is involved in magickal creation. Magick is inherently holistic; you can't separate body from mind.

You should also avoid magick when under the influence of any negative emotion. This can be jealousy, fatigue, job stress, hatred, anger, or fear. The circle magnifies all energy within it and these are not emotions you want made stronger.

the craft of the wise

It's not by accident that we Witches refer to our spiritual life as a craft. By now you should be getting a feel for Witchcraft as a fine art, not a shotgun full of magick splattering haphazardly all around you. Witchcraft is an art that just happens to carry with it awesome responsibility and a never-ending commitment to learning and improving one's self and one's skills. It's an unending quest for knowledge that can be turned into wisdom through experience, and it means eternal devotion to the service and seeking of our deities.

In this chapter you'll get a chance to put some of the skills you've been working on to use, helping you to get a feel for successful energy manipulation in an atmosphere of "harm none." Please note that when we speak of energy manipulation, we are not speaking of negative magick or the manipulating of someone's free will. We are talking about shaping and bending the energies around us to put into our magickal will.

As you work through this chapter, you may find you have an innate talent for some of these exercises, and that could make beginner's work seem too easy. Just remember that none of us will ever master all the magickal processes available to us, and where someone else may shine, you may wither. Be patient, do your best, and don't allow yourself to get frustrated.

the ancient art of healing

Witches heal.

I always feel a strong sense of pride when I run across that statement on a bumper sticker or see someone wearing it on a T-shirt. Healing has always been the greatest service a Witch can perform to honor her deities. By helping another person become healthy—physically, emotionally, or spiritually—you're making a real difference in someone's life. It's an unselfish act into which you pour energy for the good of someone else, and this helps to deepen our connection to the land and its sacredness.

The healing skills of the local wise woman in European villages caused many of them to be brought up on charges of Witchcraft. Still, Witches, both male and female, passed herb lore down to their children or apprentices, making the art of healing others with plants and nature's energies their primary function in many communities.

Many healing techniques that are hands-on and involve the transfer of energy to and from the patient are beyond the ability of most newcomers to the Craft. You may be gifted in this area, and what I just told you may not apply to you, but be aware that not every Witch is gifted in every skill. At the risk of sounding redundant, it requires hard work and practice.

The simplest healing techniques involve the projection of energy you draw into yourself from up above or the earth below, then taking that energy and mentally seeing it surround your patient in an egg of white pure light. You can assist in the healing of plants, trees, animals, and people this way.

Remember, if you don't have a license to practice medicine, you should never give medical advice or encourage anyone to rely solely on magickal healing. Magickal cures are best used in tandem with the care of a medical professional, many of whom are now starting to embrace the old remedies within their modern practices. Just because a treatment is natural does not mean it won't interfere with or be contraindicated by a prescription drug.

Herbalism is a huge study all on its own and I'll only touch on it briefly here. Knowledge of herbs will be useful to you right away, but leave crafting herbal remedies to others until you are more experienced. For now, practice healing through visualization and by raising and sending energy, two of the six magickal skills discussed in detail in the previous chapter. If you've skimped on practicing them, your healing skills will be weak or could even rebound on you.

magickal herbalism and that scottish play

When non-Witches think of herbal brews and potions, they often reflect on the opening scene of Shakespeare's *Macbeth*, in which three classically hideous old women are stirring up trouble over a large, smoking cauldron, tossing in such unpleasant things as eye of newt and tongue of dog. (By the way, the latter is just the herb known as houndstongue, often used in spells to keep secrets and ensure silence.)

While a complete discussion of magickal herbalism lies outside of this work (there are several good books devoted to that subject in depth, see appendix 5), we will touch on it briefly.

Witches don't make living sacrifices. Any item you see listed in a spell that sounds like it comes from part of an animal is usually an herb's old folk name. Use your common sense to decide if it's a harmful spell. If a recipe calls for horse hairs, that's one thing; if it asks for the ears or tail, that's altogether a different issue.

Witches rarely gather herbs in the wild. Unless you're an expert botanist, it's just too risky. Mother Nature guards her deadly babies by making many of them look like a benign plant. It's best to grow your own or get them from your local occult shop or through mail order (see appendix 3).

Some poisonous plants have their uses in magick, but they must be handled with care. And don't think just because a spell uses a toxic plant that it is hopelessly negative. You may use yew to contact a deceased relative, or poison ivy for protection. The Witches who use these plants know these precautions:

- Wear thick gardening gloves and eye protection. A face mask is helpful, too.

- Pick only a small portion of the poisonous part of the plant and slip it into a plastic bag that can be sealed.

- Do not burn the plant. The fumes can cause a deadly reaction inside your lungs.

- Never leave the plant lying around where a child or pet could find it.

- Never ingest any herb in any form unless you know without any doubt that it is harmless and you are not allergic to it.

- Don't try using poisonous plants until you get a firm understanding of magickal herbalism.

- Recognize that natural and safe are not synonymous terms and that even the most benign-looking plant may have a chemical structure that can cause damage to vital organs.

Some of the more common herbs you will work with as spell catalysts have been associated with their magickal properties since at least the Middle Ages. They work well for almost everyone, and they rarely cause harm unless you have an unexpected allergic reaction. Appendix 1 features a table of many common herbs and their properties.

At this point in your training, don't worry about how the herbs will be empowered or used within the framework of a spell. Your job right now is to get to know the properties of common herbs. You do this by holding the herb in your receptive, or nondominant, hand. (This would be the one opposite of the one you use to write.) You can also hold it between your palms or hold it close to the psychically sensitive brow chakra (see page 124) in the lower center of your forehead. As you increase your skill in transferring energy into magickal objects, you will be able to sense a change within the object, a change created by energy actually stimulating the molecules to move faster and to absorb your magickal will.

Keep your Book of Shadows nearby so you can record your impressions. Not all of each herb's magickal properties are listed in appendix 1, and a few will share an affinity with your personal energy and may reveal to you correspondences that would not work for other Witches. It's important that you discover these for yourself. Again, I repeat, Witchcraft is hard work, and it is never a quick fix for your troubles.

You can do these same energy experiments with various stones. They tend to be harder to find and identify, but any reputable lapidary or occult shop should have a selection of low-cost, polished stones for you to try. You can also get them mail order (see appendix 3). Stones are sometimes easier to read than herbs, and even if you don't get a sense of their magickal properties right away, you will have little trouble feeling their living energy pulsating in your palm.

Resist the urge to use gemstones set in jewelry. What you will pick up on will not be the energy of the stone, but of the person who once owned and wore the jewelry. This is known as the art of psychometry, or reading an object's past by touch, and it is a lesson for later in your Craft career.

For now, try your hand at opening communication with the common stones listed in appendix 1.

simple candle magick

Candle spells are a popular and easy way for the newcomer to Witchcraft to learn her craft. Many occult shops carry elaborately made candles preprogrammed to suit almost any need or desire. Many come in shapes, like people for healing, couples for love magick, or with pictures of desires on glass candleholders. Candles are easy to work with compared to other forms of magick, and the transformative powers of fire as it consumes an empowered candle make connecting with the visualization much easier.

A word of warning: never leave any burning candle unattended. It doesn't matter how deep the glass that encloses it is or how sure you are that your cat will not jump up on the table for a closer look. If you will be closing your eyes for more than a moment or two, leaving the room, or if you have curious children and pets, you should either forgo candle magick, or put it off until a safer time and place can be found.

Testing your power

Try playing with your personal power by cupping your hands around a candle's flame. Keep them as close as you can to the candle without risking a burn. Gaze into the flame while you visualize energy being channeled up from the earth and through your hands. Try to affect the way the candle burns. Will the flame to bend left, then bend right. Cause it to grow smaller or flare higher.

You may notice some success on your first try, but don't wear yourself out. After thirty minutes or so, stop for the day and try again after you're well rested and ready again to be a clear channel for magickal energy.

Words of power

As you hone your candle manipulation skills, you can also begin to experiment with words of power, short rhyming couplets or quatrains that express out loud your magickal intent. Follow these guidelines if you want to try your hand with words of power:

- The words should always be in the present tense, as if your goal is already manifest.

- Having your words rhyme makes them easy to remember. Rhymes also tend to create their own rhythms, which will help lull your mind into a deeper state of consciousness for magick.

- Never dictate to the universe how your spell is to manifest. Like any other energy, magick follows the path of least resistance and may have an easier way to reach you than the one you expect. By dictating to it, you could slow down or even prevent your spell from manifesting.

- Repeated chanting of the words of power, coupled with visualization, makes them stronger.

- If you're not sure about using words of power at this time, use only visualization. Clear visualization is more important to a spell's outcome than words.

How to perform a simple candle spell

Candle spells require more than just lighting the candle, mumbling a few words, and walking away with the expectation that you've done all you need to do.

At the very least, you need to sit with the candle, gazing at its hypnotic flame while visualizing the goal you desire.

Sit in front of your candle and, when you are balanced and centered, light it. Speak words of power if you have them in mind, but in any case, visualize clear and strong images of yourself having attained your goal.

There are three ways to visualize your single-candle spell.

1. Envision a problem you seek to get rid of melting away as the candle burns down.

2. As the candle burns, envision your desire being carried off into the otherworld to begin to manifest.

3. Envision the transformative power of the fire like the burner of a stove. It is beneath your spell, building a firm foundation for its success.

You can personalize the candle by rubbing it down with olive oil and carving a name or symbol of your need into its shaft. Some candle spells are very elaborate, but you should keep them simple until you feel your magickal skills are well developed.

As you prepare your candle, keep your magick goal at the forefront of your mind. You may even create a little chant or a poem that you can say as you work with the candles. Rhythmic sounds and rhymes help us focus on our goal and raise energies.

choosing the best color for your magick

Color energy plays a major role in magick, but it won't work for you if you're slavish to the "traditional" colors when you feel your magickal instincts are being pulled in another direction.

You will note in the following list of colors that many magickal needs are listed under more than one color. This is because they are both popular for achieving a specific end.

Red

Red is the color of blood, life, regeneration, renewal, war, passion, courage, stamina, strength, lust, the full moon, and winter rites, and is used in spells where fire energy needs to be its strongest.

Orange

Orange is used in spells for attraction, friendship, planetary magick, will power, and autumn rites, and is the color of navel-area chakra or energy center. Orange draws the eye, which is why it works in spells for attraction. It also revs up the metabolism and increases the appetite.

Yellow

This is the color of creativity, mind power, intellectual pursuits, study, communication, the solar plexus region of the body, and solar magick, and it is used in spells where the element of air is prominent.

Green

Green is the color of balance, Mother Earth, and renewal. This is used for spells of abundance, prosperity, personal appearance, good fortune, neutrality, fertility, and eco-magick.

Blue

Blue induces calm and is used in spells for sleep, dream incubation, peace, fidelity, loyalty, healing, and the waxing moon, and for spells in which the water element is needed.

Violet

Violet is used to enhance spirituality, opening your eyes and heart to metaphysical mysteries. It is also useful in bringing on a deep sleep, healing serious illnesses, uncovering past lives, communicating with higher beings, and in lunar magick.

White

White is used in spells for healing, purification, fidelity, the deities, and the full moon. It is useful when you want to bring the air element into your work. White is always your best default color when you are undecided about the right color to use.

Brown

Brown candles are used in magick to heal the earth, for helping animals, for eco-magick, and in spells in which the earth element is needed.

Black

Black is not a color of evil or negativity, but is the essence of our mysteries and voids. It is associated with the crone aspect of the Goddess. It is useful in absorbing unwanted energies, winter rites, and spells in which you want to bring in the unifying fifth element of spirit.

Pink

Use pink candles for spring rites, love spells, beauty spells, and spells for peace and harmony in the home.

Silver

Silver is used for lunar magick, Goddess spells, enhancing psychic powers, seeking the inner self, and for bringing the unifying element of spirit into your spells.

Gold

Gold is used in solar magick and in summer rites. It is useful in magick for employment, prosperity, personal charisma, and wealth.

what do you do when a spell fails?

First, has your spell failed, or do you just think it has? Get out your Book of Shadows and revisit exactly what you did. Check the visualizations, your color choices, and your words of power. You may find you actually got what you asked for even if it was not what you expected. This should not embarrass you. We all make these errors, even after years of practicing the Craft. I once did a spell for personal beauty that was about six rhyming quatrains long. One of the lines asked for a "youthful face." Within two weeks of my first working of the spell, my face broke out like a teenager's, complete with acne-like blemishes.

I redoubled my efforts, but my problem only got worse. Finally, one night, as I was praying to my patron Goddess, I was suddenly smacked by the realization that I had gotten exactly what I asked for. I changed the offending line and was shortly back to myself.

I find many people have a problem with love spells. In an effort to keep the spell from manipulating anyone else's free will, the spell will often be too generic. It might ask for somebody new and interesting to notice you. Someone will notice you all right, but may never approach you or ask you out.

Spells written by others can also be problematic. Treat any spell you get from a book like an architect's blueprint. Until the house is built, you can always make changes to suit yourself. In fact, you should always personalize your spells as much as you can for best effect. In time, you will discover your best catalysts and your own strengths as a Witch. It will get easier to craft your own spells, but those occasional mistakes will always occur. They've happened to all of us, and they make for entertaining stories around the coven balefire.

There are only two reasons why a spell fails.

1. The proper effort was not put into it in the first place.

2. There is a stronger force opposing your spell.

Opposition doesn't have to come from a concerted magickal effort. It can come from no more than the will of those involved to walk their own paths through life and not bend to the desires of anyone else. There is little you can do about this type of failure, nor should you risk trying to overcome someone's free will. That path will only ultimately fail you completely because it's negative. Trust me that you don't want to go there.

When it's your own magickal effort that has not been strong enough, you should first do some divinations to try and find out where your spell is weak. Carefully consider all the implications of your visualizations and words of power. Make changes where needed. You want to make what you want as clear as possible without trying to dictate to the universe how that magick is to manifest.

That's a thin line to walk, but no one said magick was easy. If it were, we'd all be rich, beautiful, famous, and cherished by our perfect soulmates.

Remember, magick is like any other energy; it takes the path of least resistance. Trying to tell it how to manifest can cause delays or failures. Make sure your intent is clear, but also be sure you have not created a channel too narrow for your positive energies to come back to you.

The last step is to reenact the revised spell, repeatedly if necessary. You may ask others to send you good wishes of energy, but then you risk raising someone else's opposing energies. Do the spell for yourself by yourself for the best and quickest results.

Nope, magick is not easy, but if you really need and want what you ask for, then no effort should be too great.

do you still want to be a witch?

Now that you've been exposed to the basic beliefs and practices of Witchcraft, do you still feel the same about it as you did when you started reading this book? Have you been moved to learn more, or is just knowing the basics enough for you? The choice is yours and there are no rights or wrongs. We each must follow the spiritual path that resonates most deeply within us.

Can you accept that Witchcraft is lots of hard work and that no priest or priestess is going to do your work for you? The most successful Witches are the ones who work hard to find what they want and need. They don't expect it be handed to them. If they have a question, they find a way to obtain the answer.

There is a hunger for basic Craft and magickal information, which, fortunately, is easy to feed in today's open atmosphere. When I first begin my Craft studies there was a dearth of resources, and hiding our beliefs in the broom closet was almost an expectation.

finding more answers (and questions)

Thank Goddess, that period of strict secrecy is behind us. Only a decade ago, it was not a good idea—it was even dangerous—to proclaim aloud one's Pagan affiliation outside of small, trusted groups. Today, there are experienced magicians, Witches, Wiccans, and Pagans in almost every city and town across North America and western Europe. Many are open about their faiths, feeling as free to express their beliefs out loud as others do.

There are many more sources for learning, too. There are excellent books, groups, periodicals, federations, teachers, and other resources that were only a dream even a decade ago. Many people who operate occult shops or metaphysical bookstores have been in the Craft for decades and can help answer your questions or recommend books and resources for study. They may even maintain a bulletin board of contacts in your area. In other words, you have hundreds of resources to turn to for assistance—resources that are faster and easier to reach than you might think.

The Internet is, as you would expect, a great source for networking and information. There are Web sites, chat rooms, news groups, vendors, periodicals, and a host of other sites that explore magick and Paganism from every angle and viewpoint. They are brimming with lively debate from interesting personalities. If you do not own a computer, your local library or public university probably has one you can use for free to browse the Internet. See the listing in appendix 3 of this book for the addresses of Web sites of popular Pagan educational and networking organizations, as well as information on retailers of ritual and magickal supplies.

There are three tips to remember to give yourself the best chance of receiving an answer if you have a question to address to specific Pagan author, publisher, artist, or organizer.

- Use e-mail rather than regular mail.
- Provide an SASE or IRC when using regular mail.
- Make your query as specific as possible.

Most artists and volunteers for nonprofit organizations hold down other full-time jobs and, with life's other demands, have little time for letter writing. Check out a publisher's, organization's, or periodical's Web site for the e-mail addresses of writers and artists whose work you admire.

My e-mail address appears below. I'm always glad to hear from others who are interested in Witchcraft. I try to respond to all messages that appear in my inbox. Just be aware that my backlog of unanswered items can trail back for months.

e-mail: edainmccoy@yahoo.com

Web site: www.edainmccoy.com

If you write via regular mail to a business or to any person unknown to you, you should always enclose a self-addressed stamped envelope or international reply coupon. You should follow this rule both in and out of the Pagan world. It is a matter of both courtesy and economic reality. The cost of hundreds of envelopes, sheets of paper, ink, and stamps makes answering large numbers of letters without return postage cost prohibitive.

To make answering a query easier, you should word your question clearly, noting a specific page number if you are asking about a passage in a book. I think most of us who write Pagan or magick books enjoy hearing about our readers' lives. We often learn something from them too. But when you're seeking specific information, ask for the specific information, making sure it is something that can be answered within the confines of a brief letter.

I get presented with lots of blanket questions that read along the lines of, "Tell me everything you know about Witchcraft." These types of general queries just can't be covered in a letter. They frustrate me because I wish I could do more, and they frustrate the letter writer who really wants to know or they wouldn't have taken the time to write. I usually reply to these types of letters with a list of books I think might help that person get started on a serious course of study, for that is the the only sensible answer.

coming out of the broom closet

Over the course of your studies, not all of your interactions will be with other Witches and Pagans or even with other souls understanding of your path. As you continue to study and practice Witchcraft, it will be up to you as to how open you want to be with others about your beliefs. Your choice will be influenced by many factors including your family's feelings, the character of your community, and your personal comfort level.

By choosing any form of Witchcraft as your religion and marking yourself in public as such, you will face prejudices from those who do not understand your faith and do not want to understand. These attacks may come in the form of verbal abuse or threats, or may even put you in physical danger from bigots, zealots, and anyone else who just likes picking on the little guys. And don't underestimate anyone's spiritual dogmatism. Even the brightest and best of people can lose all perspective when it comes to religion. You will have to learn to pick your battles and to tread with care through your daily life.

There is, of course, a middle ground between being an in-your-face Witch and cowering in the back of your broom closet waiting for the Witchhunters to cart you off to the stocks. That middle ground is just living your life as an example of a person who embraces kindness and compassion and who harms none. That is what is expected of Witches by other Witches.

I found that allowing someone to get to know me before they are privy to my personal spiritual beliefs works best—and I do not consider this to be hiding my religion. Holding back personal information until you feel comfortable sharing it is expected in other arenas. Why should your religion be handled differently? Think about how you've expressed your spiritual self in the past. For instance, when was the last time you donned religious jewelry and announced your beliefs in detail to people you met before you even gave them your name?

Common sense.

If you live in a small, conservative community or in the Bible Belt, you will encounter more resistance than you would in large cities or in regions known for their liberality. Wearing Pagan symbols, such as a pentacle—a five-pointed star within a circle that symbolizes Wicca—has landed young people in the courts, where they've had to fight to confirm that we all have the right to wear the symbols of our faith or nobody does. Many of these brave souls aren't sure when the last bang of the gavel of civil rights hits the judge's table if they've gained anything. Learn to pick your battles.

Common sense.

I was raised by a father who believed that one's spirituality was a private matter between and individual and the divine. He was a minister in a left-wing sect of mainstream Christianity. Often he observed the in-your-face zealots of various faiths and asked, "Who is it they're trying to convince?" If you have any doubts about who you're trying to convince, keep your studies to yourself for a while until you either develop the courage of your convictions, or until you decide which spiritual path is the one you want to tread through this life.

Common sense.

When people know you, and have a feel for the ethics by which you live your life, they're much more likely to be accepting of your spiritual life when you begin to share it.

Common sense.

People fear most what they don't understand, and there will always be some people you can't educate and minds you can't open. In these cases, a wise Witch will keep his feelings to himself and wait for a better time to discuss with others what he believes and what he does to honor his concept of deity.

Again, common sense.

time and tests for introspection

In some traditions, it is a requirement for the postulant to ask three times to be admitted. In some traditions, the priest or priestess must ask the newcomer three times to join the ritual circle. In either case, only on the third attempt is that person admitted into the circle.

This chapter constitutes my asking you for the second time if you really want to be a Witch. It takes the circuitous route by asking you many other questions, which, when looked at as a whole, will give you, or you and your teachers, some deep insights into how much you really want this and how you will fare spending the rest of this lifetime walking the path of the Old Religion.

The first thing to keep in mind is that there are no right or wrong answers. This test is purely subjective. I developed it to help me assess the progress of my own Craft students prior to their initiations. The test has gone through many incarnations and has been flexible enough to fit many teaching situations. I usually give a copy of the questions to my students after initiation so they can refer to it later on, when introspection about their direction in the Craft is needed or desired.

Pay attention to your answers. Don't respond with what you think someone else would want to hear, but with what is in your heart and soul. Some of your answers will be mixed, and a simple yes or no will not suffice. Write the questions and your answers in your Book of Shadows, using it like a journal to explore your feelings in depth.

No one expects that you will know all the answers to these questions. Not all questions have been addressed in this books, and others won't be presented until the next chapter. At this point it's only important that you try to answer as best you can. Witches must learn to listen to the inner voice we call intuition. Start stretching your intuitive abilities right now.

If you decide you want to go farther into Witchcraft, make a note to yourself to come back to these questions after your year and day and see if and how any of your responses have changed.

100 questions for newcomers to Witchcraft

1. Do you get upset with repeating lessons you think you've already learned?

2. Do you feel defensive if someone instructs you?

3. Is the thought of a never-ending journey into wisdom more than you can bear to think about?

4. Do you have the strength to be different? Is your difference meant to annoy family and friends? If not, how far would you go with the courage of your convictions?

5. Have you ever had the experience of being a minority with all its attendant prejudices and persecutions? Even if you haven't, how well do you think you would you handle such experiences as a Witch?

6. Do you get defensive in group situations of any kind if you feel your way is right? Is there room in you for compromise? If so, where would you draw the line over which you will not cross?

7. What do you see as the major differences between someone who calls himself a Witch and someone who calls himself a Wiccan? What about a Pagan? Can someone be a Witch but not Wiccan?

8. What are the origins of Wicca and from where does the word derive?

9. How has Witchcraft been diabolized by the mainstream religions?

10. What, if any, are the differences between religion and spirituality?

11. Do you see Witchcraft as a religion or as a spirituality?

12. Can you explain the symbolism of the pentacle?

13. What is the significance of a pentagram with its apex pointed upward? What about a pentagram pointed downward?

14. Can you foresee any time when a Pagan would wear the pentacle in a downward position? Why or why not?

15. What is meant by the term "solitary" or "solitaire" when applied to a Witch?

16. What is the traditional number of members for a coven and why?

17. What is the difference between a degreed or hierarchical tradition or coven and an egalitarian or priestly one?

18. What is the difference between a Wiccan tradition and eclectic Wicca?

19. Have you found at least one cultural pantheon that you're interested in learning more about? What is it and why? How much do you already know about that culture?

20. Give a brief description of the attributes of each of the four elements.

21. What is the fifth element? What are its attributes? In a circle, where can it be located?

22. For each element, name at least three corresponding ritual tools.

23. What is a self-initiation? Is it valid? Why or why not?

24. Why do you think some form of formal initiation is important to functioning as a Pagan?

25. What is the length of the traditional period of study before initiation?

26. What is the Wiccan/Pagan Rede?

27. What is the Threefold Law?

28. Does the Threefold Law apply in nonmagickal situations? *Are* there nonmagickal situations?

29. How does magick work?

30. Name the six prerequisites for successful spellcraft.

31. Name the six skills needed for successful magick.

32. When do you feel it's appropriate to work magick for others? How do the Rede and the Threefold Law influence your decision?

33. What is meant in magick by charging, enchanting, and empowering?

34. Is magick a necessary part of Paganism? Can magick work outside of Paganism?

35. Is magick a spiritual pursuit? Why or why not?

36. Is magick a religious pursuit? Why or why not?

37. How does psychic development relate to magickal practice?

38. Are making magick and working a spell synonymous activities? Why or why not?

39. Is divination magick? What is the role of divination within magick?

40. Why is it important to do a divination prior to working a spell?

41. Why and how do we use ritual in Pagan religious expression? Why and how do we use ritual in magick?

42. Why do we not touch another Witch's tools without permission?

43. What is an athame? A bolleen? A scourge? Name and describe as many magical tools and their associations as you can.

44. Why is a circle cast for magick and ritual?

45. Do you feel a circle is always necessary for magick or divination?

46. Do you feel there's only one right way to cast and close a circle? Why or why not?

47. Why are timepieces not generally permitted inside the circle?

48. Why is it not wise to break the circle once it is cast?

49. What is deosil? Is it always positive?

50. What is meant by widdershins? Is it always negative?

51. Which direction, deosil or widdershins, would you use for a spell to banish a bad habit? For invoking protection? For gaining a lover?

52. What are the sabbats? Explain in detail the significance of at least one.

53. What is an esbat?

54. Is it permissible to work magick on the sabbats? The esbats? Which kind of magick can you work on the sabbats or esbats, and for whom can it be done?

55. What is meant by "as above, so below"?

56. What is meant by macrocosm and microcosm? How does this relate to Wiccan practices and beliefs?

57. What do Pagans believe happens to them after death?

58. What do you feel are the pros and cons of memorized rituals?

59. Why is the study of mythology important to understanding Paganism?

60. What is a Book of Shadows and how did it get its name?

61. What were the Burning Times and why is this label misleading?

62. What is your personal concept of the divine?

63. How do the deities relate to magick?

64. Why do you think many Pagans have patron deities?

65. What is the Ceremony of Cakes and Ale? What is a libation?

66. What is meant by "skyclad"?

67. What is the significance of each of the three phases of the moon?

68. How is astrology used in Pagan practice?

69. What is the Great Rite?

70. On which day of the week would a fertility spell best be worked? A spell for protection? For romance? For health? For mental prowess? For protecting one's children?

71. Name the planets associated with each day of the week.

72. How would you rework or reword a spell to make it more compatible with what at first seems to be an inauspicious lunar phase?

73. What kind of spells would you initiate on a full moon? A new moon? A lunar eclipse?

74. How would you expect a solar eclipse to impact a spell for prosperity?

75. How would you deflect negative energy which had been sent your way? How would you protect yourself against reinfestation?

76. What instincts tell you that you may wish to use magick to protect yourself?

77. Explain the magickal significance of at least three colors.

78. What is a catalyst in magick?

79. What knowledge do you currently possess of specific Witchcraft traditions? Which ones interest you most, and why?

80. Why are the terms "black magick" and "white magick" not popular with Witches?

81. What is visualization? Why is it important to magick?

82. How do you plan your visualization in relation to spellwork?

83. Are there any times, situations, or frames of mind when magick should not be worked?

84. What is meant by centering, and how is it done?

85. What is eco-magick?

86. What is grounding and why is it important to do it after engaging in magick or ritual?

87. Describe how you raise and send energy towards a magickal goal? How do you envision it working?

88. Do Pagans pray? Do you pray? Why or why not?

89. What is the meaning of the phrase "so mote it be"? How is it used?

90. What, if any, is the difference between evocation and invocation?

91. What are the strengths you bring to the Craft? What are your weaknesses? What, if anything, are you going to do with this knowledge?

92. What type of challenges do you expect to face if you embrace the Craft as your spiritual path in this life?

93. Do you see your role in the Craft changing over time?

94. Do you resent being told a "better" way to do something? How do you handle it when you're given a "better" way that does not resonate with you?

95. Do you work and play well with others?

96. Do people from different social, economic, or ethnic backgrounds make you uncomfortable? Did you come from a family with prejudices? Do you embrace any of them yourself?

97. Do you believe one culture is superior to another and that only their traditional magick is "correct"?

98. Do you want to serve your community or have it serve you?

99. Can you turn knowledge into wisdom through experience, or would you rather be a "book Witch"?

100. What else do you want to learn? Where do you go from here? How will you get there?

taking your first steps into witchcraft

Hail and welcome, young dedicant!

Yes, that's you . . . at least it is for now.

This is also my asking you for the third time if you want to be a Witch. Three. The magickal number. The power number. The number of completion.

What do you think? Have you made up your mind about Witchcraft yet, or do you need more time? There's no rush. We're not going anywhere, and there are lots of other books and many Web sites you can explore for more information.

So, do you want to be a Witch? I mean do you really, really, *really* want to be a Witch, or do you want to play at being a Witch? Do you want a new religion to practice, or do you just want to do something to shock your family, friends, or co-workers? Think about it.

How do you feel about becoming a Witch? Anxious? Peaceful?

The road of the Witch is not an easy one; there are many roadblocks across the path and many more enchanting things to distract us from our work. Still, an amazing number of us keep stumbling along, sure that what we'll find at the end of a long life in search of and in service to our deities will be worth the effort.

You will grow closer to the deities as you progress through your studies. You learn their many names, and which ones want to partner with you and which do not. They will all toss surprising challenges across your path to test your resiliency and your capacity to work with the forces of nature. As your skill level grows, so will the difficulties of the challenges. None are meant to harm you, but rather are intended to make you think, reason, and then act, in ways that "harm none."

The first thing to remember is that Witchcraft is a *religion*. The worship of the God and Goddess is our primary function. We accept magick because we have not rejected the natural energies upon which it is based, nor do we feel that being cast in the image of our deities disempowers us. It's just the opposite.

The second thing to remember is that the terms "magician" and "Witch" are not always the same thing. Folk magick is the inheritance of all people. Anyone can practice it, and many do with good results. If you find you are reluctant to give up your current religion for the sake of doing magick, then, by all means, don't.

beyond your year and a day

There are always new things to learn and new ways of looking at or doing something that's already familiar to you. You can become a priest or priestess, a leader, a healer, a seer, an elder, or anything else to which you aspire. Just keep in mind that this means more hard work.

It also depends on the tradition in which you wish to practice. Some have strict standards about how one passes through the hierarchy of their circles. These usually involve a combination of time passing and level of learning.

The same is true if you are a solitary Witch and want to attain these titles. Time and study and living a magickal lifestyle in which you feel all things are possible are the only ways to advance.

if you need more help

I feel the best-educated Witches are both well read and have worked with several different teachers. I will be the first to say that you cannot learn everything from books. At some point you will need interaction with or guidance from an experienced Witch. There is an old magickal adage that says, "When the student is ready, the teacher will appear." I would venture to add, "But you must seek your teacher lest you not notice him when he appears."

Expose yourself to as many different Wiccan and Pagan ideas as you can to decide what works for you. Even if you find a worthy teacher, you will probably find that she wants you to read many of these books anyway, as well as lots of texts on mythology, history, science, and culture.

Don't get overly anxious and take just any teacher who comes along. Know what you want from him before you seek him out, and be mentally and emotionally prepared for your lessons. The late British priestess Sybil Leek wrote in *The Complete Art of Witchcraft* that, before embarking successfully on a study of the Craft, you must "see to your own house first." You must have some stability and order in your life, and not be worrying about making it from day to day, before you can make the kind effort that magick requires to be successful. This is why magick is never our solution of first resort when things go wrong. The Witch is simply not centered and balanced and in the right frame of mind to focus the magick on the need.

be careful what you wish for

Deciding to become a Witch is a major decision. You'll not only be changing religions but your lifestyle as well. You will become attuned daily to the phases of the moon and attempt to walk in harmony with all creation. Living this way makes a pretty picture in your head right now, I know. But this life of connection to all living things is not as easy as it sounds. The modern world makes a harmonious union with nature difficult at best.

You may want to meditate on or dream over your spiritual choices. You can always put it aside come back to it later. As I stated in chapter 1, I read my first Craft book in 1972, but didn't commit to a year and a day of study until almost ten years later. This religion is not for everyone. It demands great self-control, a keen sense of self-responsibility, and the determination of a bull terrier to seek out resources.

The magickal part of the Craft cannot be mastered in a day any more than any other skill can. Successful Witchcraft requires that you have a solid emotional and mental foundation on which to build. Negative emotions or a distressed mental state will send your energies awry and make you all the more desperate to succeed. Desperation is not a positive emotion and will not yield favorable outcomes for your spells and rituals.

If you've decided this religion is not for you, I thank you for taking the time to read this little book. Knowledge is a precious gift and is never wasted. What you know about Witchcraft may come in handy someday. I wish you well on whatever spiritual journey you do choose, and someday we will meet again when we return to our creator.

For those of you who have decided to pursue Witchcraft as your chosen religion, get that Book of Shadows in which you've hopefully been recording thoughts and ideas since chapter 1, and write today's date on the top of the page. This begins your year and a day of serious study. This book is merely your introduction, a primer for a basic understanding of the Wiccan path. Ahead of you lie many years of study, growth, and wisdom to be absorbed and, perhaps, passed on to students of your own someday.

witchcraft is hard work

A Witch becomes a Witch only through his personal efforts of study and practice. Period. By tradition it takes a year and a day of reading, working, and learning to know and love the deities you seek to connect with and worship. After a year and a day, it is acceptable to do an initiation and call yourself a Witch, Wiccan, or Pagan.

Just because you call yourself a Witch, Wiccan, or Pagan does not mean that your learning process has stopped, though. It has just begun. You've only scratched the surface of the door that opens to all worlds. To pass through it at will takes much more skill and effort.

There will be more branches on your learning tree than you'll have time for in only a year, so many things will have to be put aside and delved into later. This first year is for mastering the basic concepts, divination, and basic magick.

Self-initiations are accepted by most Pagans as a valid expression of your commitment to your Craft. No one will challenge you as long as you display the knowledge expected of an initiate with a year-and-a-day's study behind her. However, please keep one concept in mind. If you wish to call yourself a part of any particular tradition or subsect within Paganism, you will be expected to study with someone within that tradition and to be initiated into it by one of its priests or priestesses.

There are many good books on basic Witchcraft lining the bookstore shelves. Most of them provide lots of practical exercises that enhance the text and cover your questions in depth. Appendix 5 provides the names of some of the books best known to me. Look for books by Silver Raven-Wolf, Scott Cunningham, Laurie Cabot, Raymond Buckland, Marion Weinstein, Vivianne Crowley, Starhawk, Gerina Dunwich, Ann Moura, Dorothy Morrison, and Stewart and Janet Farrar to start. If your local bookstore cannot find these authors for you, you may want to search on online bookstores and Pagan Internet vendors such as www.azuregreen.com.

networking: study groups and covens

The question I'm most often asked is where someone can find a local coven to take them in. In fact, there have been so many queries over the years that I was inspired to write *The Witch's Coven* (Llewellyn Publications, 2003) to address the issue.

Neither I nor any other practicing Witch or Pagan knows who forms and works in covens, even within our our own cities and towns. Even if we did know, we would not be at liberty to compromise their privacy or safety by making their information public. To find a coven you have to hunt, and even then it may be the wrong match for you, even though the ways in which you practice are all perfectly valid.

Another truth is that no coven will ever come seeking you. There are many established covens that don't even want new members. The only exception to this are some teaching covens who would take you into an outer circle with other newcomers. Your best bet is to find other solitaries and form your own group if this is the way you wish to worship. And don't tell me you're the only Witch within fifty miles. I know from experience that, once the word is out, you can draw a nice crowd. Even if you don't find people with whom you wish to merge your personal energies during a ritual, you will have made new friends and valuable Craft contacts.

I can't stress enough that not every coven is right for every Witch any more than every church or synagogue is right for every Christian or Jew. Being in the wrong group can be worse than being in none at all. Please refrain from jumping into the first group that asks you before you've had time to check them out and learn how, why, and whom they worship.

seek and ye shall find

No twenty-first-century Witch who's making serious inquiries about groups should fail in making connections with like-minded others. Twenty years ago, I would have commiserated with you. Today, resources and networking opportunities are as abundant as bumble bees in spring. You can find them in the many Pagan publications that are now sold on newsstands in larger bookstores, in the backs of books on magickal or Pagan topics, at the local Unitarian Universalist church, through national antidefamation organizations, on bulletin boards at occult shops or health food stores, from the owner of the local metaphysical bookstore, in advertisements in alternative lifestyle publications, and online using the Internet (see appendix 3 for more details).

The best attitude to have when seeking resources and contacts is to always assume you are not the only Witch around. I've met other Pagans and Wiccans by leaving notes on cars with obviously Pagan bumperstickers, and once I met someone by making a joke about spell casting, which fell on the ears of someone who I suspected knew how spells were cast.

So, let's say after some legwork and effort on your part, you finally meet another Pagan soul, and you are as ecstatic as a child at Christmas. This is a great event in your Craft life, but it also may be a learning opportunity. Never assume that the first person you meet who claims an interest in alternative religious practice is your last and only chance of having a Pagan or Wiccan friend. Earth- and nature-based spiritual practices are among the fastest growing religions in both North America and western Europe. Take your new friend and use your joint efforts to widen your circle of contacts. You can never have too many friends and you can never have enough threads connecting to you to the web of Wicca.

I started out working exclusively with my best friend, but after a couple of years, we went our separate ways in Paganism, yet remained the best of friends. This is because we recognized that the Craft is not a one-size-fits-all religion, and we each felt the need to follow various paths within our own ethnic heritage. She joined a Scottish-based group, while I joined an eclectic, Irish-based tradition.

You should also try to attend Pagan events or gatherings whenever possible. Sometimes there are local coffeehouses that host weekly or monthly Pagan gatherings. Some covens will have an open circle once or twice a year with the goal being not just to attract the newcomers but also to put the ugly rumors about Witchcraft to rest.

You may also want to travel, either alone or with your new friends, to one of the large Pagan festivals or gatherings. These are well advertised on the Internet and in Pagan magazines and most often occur around the eight sabbats. These will expose you to the full spectrum of the Pagan-Wiccan-Witchcraft rainbow and will help you widen your circle even farther.

Now that you've connected with the Wiccan web, you should focus on your desire for a coven and narrow your objectives without sacrificing anyone within this circle of contacts you've worked hard to create. You can have lots of Pagan friends, but you probably have fewer good matches if you're looking to find or form a coven or study group. Not everyone works well together, either because their energies just don't blend well or because they have different spiritual needs.

Make a list of the things that are really important to you, such as the focus of your study, the culture in which you wish to worship, the ethics you wish to embrace, the type if ritual dress you prefer, and where and how often you want to meet with a group. Leave off the list anything you don't feel is vital to your spiritual happiness. Allow what's on the list to be your holy grail and go after what you want like a knight on a quest. There is nothing wrong with seeking what you need spiritually, and everything wrong with settling for things you know will only make you—and the group you join—miserable in the end.

Make the things you really need and want your priority and be flexible with the rest. Be prepared to hear about all sorts of essentials and must-haves from others. We all have a few in mind, and it's doubtful that any are wrong. They are unique to each person who seeks a group. You'll find some people, particularly women, who prefer to worship only a goddess and never a god. You'll find others who want only a Celtic or Germanic focus, never Greek or Roman. Some people want a strict hierarchy with well-defined group leaders, others prefer an egalitarian situation where all participants take on the leadership roles from time to time. Some have a specific tradition they know about or have read about that they want to follow, and no other will do, while others love the mind-expanding experience of eclectic Wicca in which all deities are embraced. Others will want to teach newcomers, while still others feel out of their element in this role. Some people are only comfortable around those in their own age or ethnic group, and others prefer a multigenerational, multiethnic milieu. Some people are natural crusaders and have to have an ongoing cause—such as the environment or antidefamation—to make them feel a group is worthwhile, while others just want a quiet, little circle to call their spiritual family.

Once you have a core group you feel can work well together, start off as a study group. All of you should feel free to discuss your needs and ideas in a nonjudgmental manner, just to see how they might work together. If things go well for a few months as you talk and study together, you might start to experiment with ritual. If the ritual goes well, you may have the basis for a wonderful coven. Within a year, you can be making great magick together and building a true spiritual family.

begin your quest for the right tools

Ritual tools were mentioned briefly earlier in the book, but now we'll look at them more closely. There are numerous resources for obtaining a set of ritual tools, and there should be no rush to get them. If you work for a year and a day with a single teacher or within one specific teaching coven, someone may give you one of the tools.

There are no rules which say you must have a full set of highly empowered tools to practice the Craft. You will find you acquire new ones as your skills grow and your interests change. Start your search without any sense of hurry and the right tools will find you. As you begin your quest, keep the following points in mind:

- Never haggle over the price of ritual tools. This is said by some to offend the elemental beings who inhabit the cardinal direction you wish the tool to represent. If something is too expensive for you, then just leave it alone for now.

- Many tools can be made yourself. If you can make some, then do so while keeping in your mind a visualization of you and the tool working in perfect harmony with one another.

- Some tools can be found on nature walks. Depending on what part of the world I've been in, I've gathered wooden staffs, crystals, red rocks, and amethyst.

- Never take a rock from its resting place or a branch attached to a tree before asking that rock or tree if you have its permission to do so. Keep quiet and focus on the tree or stone and your answers will come to you. If the answer is no, find another tree or stone that speaks to you. If you don't find one, go back to that area in a few days. Sometimes the tree will shed an unneeded branch for you, or your stone may have detached one better attuned to you. Nature knows her own. Trust her.

You have a wide range of choices when it comes to ritual tools, including some no one may have thought of before. The tools you select should feel as if they express to your the essence of their corresponding elements. You should feel a tool resonate with your own spiritual vibrations when you hold it.

Earth

- Animal pelts (if your conscience allows)
- Bowls of soil
- Bows
- Carved wood blocks
- Clay
- Clubs
- Concave shields
- Disks
- Double-headed axes
- Drums
- Hammers
- Mallets
- The metal bronze
- Necklaces
- Pentacles (a five-pointed star with its apex up placed inside a perfect circle)
- Roots
- Salt
- Sand
- Stones
- Wheels

Water

- Barrels
- Bolleens (a white-handled scythe, usually used for harvesting magickal herbs)
- Bowls
- Cauldrons
- Chalices
- Convex shields
- Cups
- Goblets
- Hollow horns
- Juice
- Paintbrushes
- Pitchers
- Rings
- Seashells
- Sickles
- Silver
- Tea and teakettles
- Tridents (also called a Neptune's staff, it has three tangs at the top)
- Wands from trees with feminine energy
- Wine, wine casks, wineglasses, and brandy snifters

Fire

- All blades forged in fire (including athames and swords)
- Candles
- Hearths
- Wands from trees with masculine energy
- Iron
- Red or orange stones
- Pikes
- Claymores
- Matches
- Flints
- Ashes
- Single-headed axes
- Torches
- Bracelets
- Solar disks (an equilateral cross in a circle)
- Brooms
- Gold
- Spears
- Lariats
- Scourges
- Whips

Air

- Arrows
- Athames and swords
- Brooms
- Brooches
- Claymores
- Copper
- Daggers
- Dirks
- Earrings
- Fans
- Feathers
- Incense
- Javelins
- Lariats
- Letter openers
- Pens and pencils
- Pikes
- Ram's horns
- Scourges
- Single-headed axes
- Slings
- Smoking pipes
- Smudge sticks
- Spears
- Staffs (much longer than a wand, but serving many of the same functions)
- Tridents, stangs (a two-pronged staff)
- Wands
- Whips
- Wind instruments

Preparing magical tools

Before using your tool in a ritual or magickal act, it must be cleansed of past psychic imprinting. Washing it, burying it overnight, and holding it and channeling all residual energies through you into Mother Earth are good ways to cleanse your new tool.

When you feel the tool has been purged of past energies, then place it to your own brow or navel chakra center and, using visualization, pour your own energy into the tool.

When you've done that, present the tool to the element to which it will corresponds. Introduce the two and, out loud, dedicate your tool as a catalyst of positive power. The words should come from your heart. Keep it simple and sincere. For instance, the athame dedication may sound something like this:

> Behold powers of air, the sylphs who in the
> four winds do blow. I present to you my
> athame to help me feel your energies and
> channel your power. Never allow me to forget
> that your generous power is a gift of the Lord
> and Lady. If this athame is ever misused, or if
> I should be so foul as to take the now-sacred
> object and use it with harmful intent, may it
> turn its power against me, and may the deities
> forsake me. As I will it, with harm to none and
> in the best interest of all, I say, so mote it be.

your year and a day

Your year and a day will go faster than you think, and no one expects you to know everything there is to know. No one knows it all, and much of what we do know, we have to struggle to accomplish. Use this time to find out what your best magickal energies are and develop them as much as you can. Some new Witches are visionaries, some are storytellers, some are musicians or poets, some excel at healing, some can travel the astral worlds with ease, and others are most at home in a magickal kitchen.

As you come to the end of this primer on the Craft, I wish you all the best in your spiritual journeys. To those of you whose curiosity and love of the unseen worlds is strong enough that you accept the challenges—yes, that's the right word—of your new spiritual and physical lifestyle, I wish you the blessings of the Lord and Lady. They will help you to find your own pathway through the pantheons and myths of Paganism, and they will hold you in the palms of their hands as you rise into the higher worlds of advanced Witchcraft.

herbs and gemstones

As I said in chapter 10, magickal herbalism and gemstones are a whole study unto themselves. The charts on the following pages are meant to give you a basic overview of the herbs and gems that have been used in magick since time immemorial. See page 136 for more information on using herbs and gems.

herbs and plants

Herb	Properties and associations
Apple blossom	Love, beauty, romance
Basil	Protection, warding
Bay	Protection
Bistort	Fertility
Cinnamon	Protection, prosperity
Clove	Protection, banishing, stopping gossip
Daisy	Divination, romance
Dill	Money, love
Eyebright	Psychic enhancement, mental prowess
Fenugreek	Money, employment
Frankincense	Warding, spirituality, raising vibrations
Garlic	Protection, guardian against thieves, healing
Ginger	Healing, success in all endeavors, money
Ginseng	Healing, beauty, lust, passion
Goldenrod	Divination enhancement
Hawthorn	Fertility, faery magick, making wishes
Hibiscus	Love, lust, psychic enhancement

Herb	Properties and associations
Holly	Lightning protection, dream spells
Honeysuckle	Love, romance, money
Hyacinth	Love, beauty
Jasmine	Love, beauty, dream spells, divination
Juniper	Protection from thieves, banishing
Knotweed	Binding spells, silences gossip
Lavender	Love, beauty, making wishes, peace, dreaming
Lemon	Lunar magick, purification, love
Lemongrass	Lust, psychic enhancement, drives away snakes
Lemon verbena	Fidelity, love, peaceful sleep, divination
Lilac	Past-life work, psychic enhancement, beauty
Maidenhair	Love, beauty
Maple	Love, abundance
Mugwort	Astral projection, protected travel, fertility
Myrtle	Fertility, peace, love, beauty
Nutmeg	Protection, fidelity, good luck
Oak	Strength, courage, stamina, fertility
Orange	Love, marriage

Herb	Properties and associations
Orris	Love, beauty
Paprika	Healing, warding
Parsley	Purification, protection
Peanuts	Fertility, prosperity
Pecan	Money, employment, success
Pepper	Protection, raising vibrations
Pine	Money, fertility, prosperity
Pineapple	Friendship, fidelity
Potato	Grounding, abundance, healing
Rose, red	Love, romance, healing
Rose, pink	Love, peace
Rose, yellow	Friendship
Rosemary	Love, remembrance, mental prowess, protection
Sandalwood	Wishes, spirituality, love, purification
Sesame	Fertility, passion, employment
Skullcap	Fidelity, peace in the home
Sunflower	Health, wishes, knowledge, abundance
Tomato	Assessing risks, love
Turmeric	Purification, marking sacred space
Valerian	Purification, protection, warding, peace

Herb	Properties and associations
Vanilla	Love, beauty, lust
Vervain	Love, beauty, purification, fidelity, money
Willow	Love, binding spells
Wintergreen	Purification, curse breaking, staying healthy
Yarrow	Remembrance, courage, banishing, psychic powers

Gemstones

Stone	Properties and associations
Amazonite	Money, success, winning games
Amethyst	Spirituality, peace, inner-plane work
Apache tear	Protection, warding
Aquamarine	Purification, psychicism, inner-peace
Aventurine	Mental prowess, luck, peace, healing
Bloodstone	Legal issues, antimiscarriage, healing
Carnelian	Friendship, attraction
Cat's-eye	Past lives, money, protection, truth
Chalcedony, white	Purification
Citrine	Peaceful sleep, psychic enhancement
Fluorite	Mental prowess, past lives
Geode	Things hidden, fertility, Goddess magick
Hematite	Grounding, healing
Jade	Healing, wisdom, health, prosperity
Jasper	Healing, beauty, skin problems
Jasper, red	Healing wounds, courage, protection

Stone	Properties and associations
Lapis lazuli	Fidelity, courage, spirituality
Malachite	Love, inner peace, success, eco-magick
Moonstone	Sleep, eco-magick, love, beauty, moon
Mother of pearl	Sleep, psychic powers, abundance, water
Obsidian	Grounding, divination, fire and earth
Onyx	Psychic self-defense
Opal	Astral work, beauty, money, well-being
Quartz crystal	Directing energy, spirituality
Rhodocrosite	Stamina, courage, chakra cleansing
Rose quartz	Love, romance, peace, consolation
Tiger's-eye	Employment, luck, stamina, divination
Topaz	Weight loss, energy, self-love, warding
Turquoise	Spirituality, beauty, protection
Tourmaline, black	Warding, psychic self-defense
Tourmaline, green	Eco-magick, beauty, brotherly love

moon signs

moon in aries

A moon occupying Aries will modify your personality by infusing it with an inner energy that never slows down. You tend to see the world through rose-colored glasses, and you like nothing better than the challenge of a major change in your life. Because you can't tolerate stagnation, you can zoom in and organize a project that doesn't seem to be moving. An Arian moon can also make you bitter over perceived wrongs, as well as snappish, tyrannical, and impatient.

moon in taurus

A moon in Taurus can make a trustworthy character out of anyone, though, Taureans like to keep that fact hidden. You harbor a secret passion for the arts, but you hate to get caught crying during the sad parts of movies. Taurean moons hate disorganization and can become slavish to the routines they've set for themselves. If not handled with care, they can become possessive. If your significant other is a Taurean moon, she may seem stubborn to you about moving the relationship along, but the words "I love you" lie just beneath the surface she so carefully guards.

moon in gemini

The lunar twins are similar to the solar twins, with the outer and inner selves vying for control. This can make you seem unpredictable to others. Your versatility makes you a true renaissance person, wanting to try everything, and comfortable at both a rock concert and the symphony. You can be a real charmer, but you also fear your superficiality, a trait which leads you to making hasty decisions you later regret. This is when the manipulative evil twin emerges and, depending on your solar sign, can cause you to either suppress or embrace this tendency.

moon in cancer

The moon-ruled sign of Cancer can play havoc on your emotions if your moon is charted in this sign. You can be critical and moody, hoping others will see you in distress and beg you to tell them what is wrong. Sometimes you don't know yourself what's bothering you; you just like to brood. On the other hand, this moon sign can bring out imagination, a love of all things homey and quiet, and it can make you a real crab if you feel those things are being threatened.

moon in leo

Someone with a moon in Leo may have an inner self that reflects all the worst traits of the sun in Leo. Lunar Leos must guard against feelings of conceit, selfishness, and arrogance. To the positive, you may find your Leo moon can bring out your creative imagination, make you willing to accept new ideas and practices, and give you a colorful personality. When someone hurts you, you have learned to smile through the tears with a stiff upper lip an Englishman would covet.

moon in virgo

A moon in Virgo creates a need to excel in areas requiring analytical thought. As with a sun in Virgo, a moon in Virgo person is often a high academic achiever, but never allows himself to step on top of other to attain his achievements. He is more likely to reach out a hand to help others climb along with him. This position can give you an eye for detail and skill at meticulous work. When the boss wants a project planned right, she comes to you. Even though you have tremendous self-discipline, you can be standoffish with those you feel don't work up to your standards. You also must look out for a sharp tongue, which you can use to cut anyone to shreds, though you regret it immediately after.

moon in libra

A Libran moon can make your inner self balanced and adaptable. Your ability to go with the flow without falling apart makes the good nature inside you hard to hide. You make an excellent diplomat because you tend to be flexible. For that reason, you make sure you hear all sides of issues, not just twice but several times, before coming to a conclusion. This can annoy your co-workers, who'd like to kick you in the rear, except they know that once you set a course, it will be the best one. Libra moons struggle with the urge to reinvent themselves periodically, a tendency you most need to curb is the occasional urge to make decisions in haste.

moon in scorpio

The inner Scorpio is a lot like outer Scorpio: secretive, jealous, and emotional. But the Scorpion moon hides these aspects of himself so effectively that no one but those nearest and dearest know these things are boiling just beneath the outer self. On the plus side, your Scorpion moons can enhance personal ambitions and help come up with creative solutions to any problem. Just check that tendency to want to sting perceived competition and you can balance these conflicting lunar traits.

moon in sagittarius

Having a moon in Sagittarius can give the outward mouse the roar of a lion. You are a steady worker, honest and open to new ideas. But woe to the one who crosses the Sagittarian moon, for Sagittarius can be relentless in the quest for revenge. Your secretive nature is your ruling force and can cause a general sense of unrest or suspicion where none is warranted.

moon in capricorn

The Capricorn moon can turn the steadiest, most trustworthy person into a puddle of pessimism. When things in life seem out of control, you fall back on your two best friends, rigidity and verbal abuse. The good points are found in Capricorn's surprising ability be a team player, wholly committed to the group's goal. You do the same in your personal relationships. When you fall in love, you feel lucky, and you partner is lucky to have you on her team for cheering on and general support. Just watch out that you don't see slights where none are intended.

moon in aquarius

An Aquarian moon gives you traits similar to those found in solar Aquarians, but yours are kept hidden while the solar personality wants to make sure it gets its due. This moon position can help you find creative solutions for problems and give you a deep tolerance for the bungles of others. However, in your search for universal truth, you're like a seesaw, first tilting one way and then another. People can sometimes find following your chain of thought draining. With these people, you must resist the urge to be snappish or to write them off as unworthy of your attention.

moon in pisces

Having a moon in Pisces enhances the psychic abilities native to both the moon and the sign. You tend to be excellent at divination. You and your fellow Piscean moons are natural psychics, who have sharply honed intuitions and are loving enough that you will often overtax yourselves to help a friend in need. Compassionate and big-hearted, you must struggle to overcome the moon's dark aspects: indecision, resistance to sharing, antisocial tendencies, depression, and discontentment.

resources

Look into local occult supply shops to find your magickal accouterments before you seek other resources. This helps support your local Craft community and provides a solid starting place for networking with others.

Every attempt has been made to make this appendix accurate at the time of publication. Remember that addresses can change, businesses can fail, books can go out of print, and periodicals can cease publication. Sometimes free catalogs find they must charge for subscriptions or raise prices to stay competitive.

Many organizations, publications, and businesses have found their way into cyberspace. Fire up those search engines on your Web browser for links to these and many other resources.

herbs, oils, tools, and other accoutrements

Aroma Vera

5310 Beethoven Street
Los Angeles, CA 90066
800-669-9514
www.aromavera.com

Write for catalog of essential oils, floral waters, dried products, aromatherapy oils, and incense censors.

Azure Green

PO Box 48-WEB
Middlefield, MA 01243-0048
413-623-2155
www.azuregreen.com

Azure Green has almost everything, including stellar customer service. Request a free catalog or order on their Web site.

Balefire

6504 Vista Ave.

Wauwatosa, WI 53213

This mailorder company carries a large stock of brews, oils, and incenses designed for specific Pagan needs such as scrying, spirit contact, and spellwork. Write for catalog.

Branwen's Cauldron

7657 Winnetka Ave. #102

Canoga Park, CA 91306

818-881-0827

www.branwenscauldron.com

Dreaming Spirit

PO Box 4263

Danbury, CT 06813-4263

Natural, homemade incense, resins, and oils, and the tools for using them. Dreaming Spirit welcomes queries about custom blends of incenses or oils. The two dollars for their catalog is refundable with your first order.

Earth Scents by Marah

PO Box 948

Madison, NJ 07940

www.members.aol.com/MarahCo/

Sellers of herbs, incenses, books, oil blends, and other tools. Send one dollar for a catalog.

General Bottle Supply

1930 E. 51st St.

Los Angeles, CA 90058

800-782-0198

www.bottlesetc.com

Write for free catalog of herb, oil, and salt bottles.

Gypsy Heaven

115 S. Main St.

New Hope, PA 18938

215-862-5251

www.gypsyheaven.com

Halcyon Herb Company

Box 7153 L

Halcyon, CA 93421

Sells not only magickal herbs, but also staffs, brooms, cloaks, drums, and other items of interest to Pagan folk. Current catalog is five dollars.

Indiana Botanic Gardens

2401 W. 37th Ave.

Hobart, IN 46342

1-800-644-8327

www.botanicchoice.com

Sells herbal health products, dried herbs, and essential oils.

Isis Metaphysical

www.isisbooks.com

A popular Denver classroom, bookstore, and supply shop.

Just Wingin' It

PO Box 20994

Riverside, CA 92516-0994

888-430-4594

www.jwi.com

Jewelry, incense, bottles, and other magickal items, both wholesale and retail.

Lavender Folk Herbal

PO Box 1261, Dept. SW

Boulder, CO 80306

Medicinal and magickal tea blends, herbs, and herbal crafts. The catalog is two dollars, but the price is refundable with first order.

Light and Shadows

Catalog Consumer Service

2215-R Market St., Box 801

San Francisco, CA 94114-1612

Write for their free metaphysical-supply catalog.

MoonScents

PO Box 1588-C

Cambridge, MA 02238

603-356-3666

www.moonscents.com

Large collection of magickal paraphernalia and books.

The Mystic Merchant

251-645-9081

www.mysticmerchant.com

Natural Impulse Handmade Soap and Sundries

PO Box 94441

Birmingham, AL 35220

205-854-9040

www.naturalimpulse.com

Sells readymade soaps made of natural oils by a company openly committed to protecting the environment.

Nimue's Garden

Body Al' Nature'l

PO Box 994

Havelock, NC 28532

252-259-1227

www.nimuesgarden.com

Homemade ritual soaps, body lotions, and other magickal beauty products for both men and women.

Pagan Pretties

866-747-7389

www.paganpretties.com

Jewelry and other odds and ends.

POTO

3324 E. 7th St.

Long Beach, CA 90804

562-438-4377

www.poto.com

POTO is short for "Procurer of the Obscure." POTO specializes in stocking or locating rare and hard-to-find occult items.

White Lightning Pentacles / Sacred Spirit Products

88 Wharf St.

Salem, MA 01970

978-744-0202

www.wlpssp.com

Sellers of books, magickal tools, herbs, incense, and other occult items.

Triple Moon Witchware

15 Powder House Circle

Needham, MA 02492

781-453-0363

www.witchware.com

Lots of jewelry and other items.

general pagan publications

Accord Magazine

Council of the Magickal Arts, Inc.
PO Box 890526
Houston, TX 77289
www.magickal-arts.org

Blessed Bee

PO Box 641
Port Arena, CA 95468
707-882-2052
www.blessedbee.com

Publications for Pagan families with younger children.

Circle Magazine

PO Box 219
Mount Horeb, WI 53572
608-924-2216
www.circlesanctuary.org

A popular, professional journal for Pagan news and gatherings, contacts, and seasonal celebration information.

PanGaia

Blessed Bee, Inc.
PO Box 641
Point Arena, CA 95468
www.pangaia.com

Pagan- and Gaia-spirituality–based publication. Professional format and artwork.

Personal Journaling

www.writersdigest.com/journaling

This relatively new magazine is devoted to personal writing. The Web site allows journalers to share their ideas and inspirations.

online networking

The Internet has exploded with Pagan and Wiccan information in proportion to booming interest. Local libraries or public universities often have connections you can use if you're not online at home. The resources listed here are national or international in scope, but hundreds of other regional, state or provincial, local, and campus organizations exist. Use a search engine to find ones not listed here.

BeliefNet

www.beliefnet.com

This unique site examines and connects people of all beliefs. BeliefNet features articles from upcoming publications and offers challenging techniques for exchange of ideas. It includes a large section on "Earth-based" religions, including a detailed listing of open covens and groups and those that are forming.

The Church of All Worlds

www.caw.org

This group has "Nests" all around the world. If there is not one in your area, they can help you start one.

Circle Guide to Pagan Groups

www.circlesanctuary.org/publications

This biennial publication lists open groups, stores, forums, and other places to network.

The Council of Magickal Arts

www.magickal-arts.org

Networking organization based in Texas. The council produces an excellent journal, *The Accord*, and is expanding its horizons all the time.

Covenant of the Goddess (CoG)

PO Box 1226

Berkeley, CA 947

www.cog.org

CoG is perhaps the largest Pagan networking organization. If there is not a group near you, they can help guide you through their program.

Covenant of Unitarian Universalist Pagans (CUUPs)

www.cuups.org

If you live in or near a large city, it's likely you have a Unitarian Universalist church near you. If they do not already have a CUUPs group, talk to someone there about what is needed to form one.

The Fellowship of Isis

PO Box 952
Tucson, AZ 8573
www.fellowshipofisis.com

The Fellowship of Isisis a networking and teaching organization based in Ireland, and maintains a presence in many other countries.

Magickal Education Convocation

www.convocation.org

News for an annual spirituality convocation in Michigan.

New Age Information Network

www.newageinfo.com

A good resource for a variety of New Age topics. Home of the *New Age Journal*.

Pagan Education Network (PEN)

PO Box 586
Portage, IN 46368
www.paganednet.org

American Pagan activist site.

PagaNet News

PagaNet Inc.
PO Box 654
Virginia Beach, VA 23466
www.paganet.org

Pagan community news, editorials, and advice.

The Pagan Federation, Canada

PO Box 832, Station T
Ottawa, ON KlG 3H8
Canada
www.pfpc.ca

The Pagan Federation, England

B.M. Box 797
London WC1N 3XX, United Kingdom
www.paganfed.demon.co.uk

The Pagan Federation, Scotland

PO Box 4251
Anstruther, Fife KY10 3YA, United Kingdom
www.paganfed.vscotland.org.uk

The Pagan Federation, South Africa

www.pfsa.org

Pagan Ireland

www.paganireland.com

Pagan Network Webring

www.paganprofiles.com

Pagan Paths IRC Chat Network

www.paganpaths.org

The Witches' Voice

PO Box 4924

Clearwater, FL 33758

www.witchvox.com

The Witches' Voice is an excellent and beautifully maintained site for the latest news and information on the Pagan world. Education, unity, and networking are the focus. Witches' Voice maintains a huge database of open circles and covens that teach or are open to new members, as well as a list of Pagan gatherings at the local level.

Witches' League for Public Awareness (WLPA)

PO Box 8736

Salem, MA 01971

www.celticcrow.com

The Witches' League for Public Awareness was first organized in the 1980s by Salem Witch, author, and activist Laurie Cabot to educate the public on Witchcraft.

glossary of common witchcraft terms

Altered state of consciousness

This is the art of taking your mind into more receptive, sleeplike levels of consciousness, while remaining awake and actively controlling the process.

Archetype

Archetypes are universal symbols. In Jungian psychology, they are inherited ideas or patterns of thought. Archetypal symbols speak to all of us in the ecumenical language of the subconscious.

Astral plane

A realm generally conceptualized as an invisible other world that overlaps and penetrates our waking senses and remains unseen from our own solid world of form.

Astral projection

The art of leaving one's body or shifting consciousness. When astral projecting, one visits other locations, realms, or times while in a trance state.

Astrology

Considered a pseudoscience in the mainstream, this is the study of the movements and placements of planets and other heavenly bodies and their influences on the lives and behaviors of human beings.

Athame

The ritual, double-edged knife often associated with the element of air and the direction of east, though some traditions attribute it to fire and south.

Aura

The life-energy field surrounding all living things.

Banishing

The act of sending away from ourselves, our ritual areas, or our homes all negative energies and beings. Similar to the less often used word "exorcism."

Balefire or bonfire

The traditional communal fire of the sabbats. The name is derived from the Anglo-Saxon word *boon* meaning a "gift" or "something extra." Even in modern times, balefires play a major role in both Pagan and non-Pagan holidays and folk celebrations. The modern word "bonfire" is synonymous with "balefire," though bonfires often have no religious significance.

Beltane

This sabbat, celebrated on May 1, is rife with fertility rituals and symbolism, and is a celebration of the sacred marriage of the Goddess and the God.

Besom

The Witch's broomstick.

Book of Shadows

Also called "Book of Lights and Shadows," this is the spell book, diary, and ritual guide used by an individual or coven. Some say the name came from having to hide the workings from church authorities, and others say it means that an unenacted spell or ritual is a mere shadow, not taking form until performed by a Witch.

Burning Times

The time from the fifteenth to eighteenth centuries when the worst Witchhunts and killings took place in Europe.

Cauldron

Linked to Witches in the popular mind, this is a primal goddess image, used like a chalice or cup. It is sometimes used to represent the element of water.

Ceremonial magick

A highly codified magickal tradition based upon kabballah, the Jewish-Gnostic mystical teachings. Also known as High Magick.

Chakra

From a Sanskrit word loosely translated as "wheel." These are the sacred, principal energy centers of the human body, the seven principal centers located at the base of the tailbone, at the navel, the solar plexus, the heart center, the breastbone, the throat, the brow, and just above the crown of the head.

Chalice

The chalice or cup is a ritual tool representing water and the west. In many western Pagan traditions, it also represents the feminine principle of creation.

Charging

The act of empowering an herb, stone, or other magickal catalyst with the energies of one's goal. Charging is synonymous with enchanting, empowering, and programming.

Circle

The sacred space wherein magick is to be worked and ritual enacted. The circle both contains raised energy until needed and provides protection for the Pagan/magician while inside.

Collective unconsciousness

A term used to describe the connection of all living things, past and present. The collective unconscious is synonymous with the terms "deep mind" and "higher self." It is believed to be the all-knowing energy source that we tap into during divination.

Consecrate

To consecrate something is to dedicate it to a sacred or higher purpose. To bless or to make holy.

Conscious mind

That part of the brain that we have access to in the course of a normal, waking day. It is the part of the mind that is critical and analytical in nature and that holds retrievable memory.

Coven

A group of Witches who worship and work together. A coven may contain any number of Witches, both male and female, but the traditional number of members is thirteen, which reflects the thirteen moons in the solar year, or three persons for each season plus a priest/ess. Also called a "circle," "sept," "touta," or "grove."

Cowan

A term Pagans give to those not following the old ways. This is similar to Jews referring to non-Jews as gentiles. It is not a derogatory word.

Dedicant

A newcomer to Witchcraft who has pledged himself to a year and a day of study in order be initiated into the Craft.

Deosil

Clockwise motion. Any moving, working, or dancing in a clockwise motion can be described as deosil. This is the traditional direction a Witch works in for creative magick or spells that seek to increase something. Many Witches open their sacred circles by moving deosil around them. Deosil is also called sunwise. Widdershins is the opposite of deosil.

Divination

The act of divining the future by reading potentials currently in motion. Divination can be done through meditation, scrying, astral projection, cards, stones, or any one of a myriad of other means.

Earth plane

A metaphor for your normal, waking consciousness, or for the everyday, solid world we live in.

Eclectic

A Witch, Wiccan, or Pagan who draws on many different cultures and traditions for her magickal and ritual ideas is called an eclectic Witch. In general, she is said not to be following any one specific Pagan tradition. Eclectic Wicca is a branch of Witchcraft not tied to any one tradition; rather it draws on many cultures.

Elementals

Archetypal spirit-beings associated with one of the four elements. Elementals are sometimes called faeries and are perceived of as inhabiting the faery realms. These are gnomes for the earth, sylphs for the air, salamanders for fire, and undines for water.

Elements

The four components once thought to make up the entire universe. These are earth, air, fire, and water, plus the fifth element of pure spirit in, of, and outside them all. Each Pagan tradition has its own specific directions, tools, and correspondences for each of these.

Esbat

A term for a lunar festival or monthly gathering of Witches. The word comes from the Old French *esbattre*, meaning "to frolic." Magick is often performed at esbats, both by individuals and groups.

Great Rite

A ritual symbolizing the sexual union or sacred marriage of the Goddess and God from whose union comes all creation. The Rite is performed by a man and women who are representative of the male and female polarities of deity. This ritual is most often performed by placing a knife (a phallic symbol) into a chalice (primal female image).

Grounding

To disperse excess energy generated during any magickal or occult rite by sending it into the earth. It can refer to the process of centering one's self in the physical world both before and after any ritual or astral experience.

Herbalism

The art of using herbs to facilitate human needs both magickally and medically. It is also known as "wort cunning." "Wort" is an obsolete word for herb, and "cunning" refers to secret knowledge.

Imbolg

A sabbat also known as Candlemas, Imbolc, or Oimelc. Imbolg, observed on February 2, is a day that honors the Virgin Goddess as the youthful bride of the returning Sun God.

Initiate

A novice who comes to the end of her year and a day of study and seeks to become initiated in Witchcraft. Some circles use this term synonymously with dedicant.

Karma

A Sanskrit word for the ancient belief that good and evil done will return to be visited on a person either in this life or in a succeeding one.

Lammas

A sabbat also known as Lughnasadh or August Eve. This sabbat celebrates the first harvest. The date is August 1 or 2 depending upon your tradition.

Law of Responsibility

This is an often-repeated collateral law to the other laws of Paganism. It simply means that if you inadvertently violate someone's free will or harm someone in any way, you will accept responsibility for your action and seek to make restitution. This, of course, does not apply in cases where you have used magick to protect yourself from someone seeking to harm you.

Litha

A name for the summer solstice, also called Midsummer. This sabbat celebrates the sun and its god at the peak of their annual cycle through the wheel of the year.

Mabon

This sabbat is named for the Welsh god Mabon. It is celebrated as a harvest festival on the autumn equinox.

Meditation

A deliberate attempt to slow the cycles per second of one's brain waves to generate a consciously controlled sleeping state.

Mysticism

The art of attempting to raise the human spirit to the place where it reaches and merges with what is known as the godhead, or source of creation.

Occult

The word "occult" literally means "hidden" and is broadly applied to a wide range of metaphysical topics which lie outside of the accepted realms of mainstream theologies. Such topics include, but are not limited to, divination, hauntings, spirit communication, natural magick, ceremonial magick, alternative spirituality, psychic phenomena, alchemy, astrology, demonology, and the study of the spiritual practices of ancient civilizations.

Old Religion

Another name for Witchcraft or Paganism, particularly as practiced in Great Britain and Ireland.

Ostara

The sabbat observed at the vernal equinox, and often referred to simply as the Spring Equinox. This sabbat celebrated the sexual union of the Goddess and God in the Norse traditions before the Celts moved this event to Beltane. Today, it is a time to celebrate new life and emerging sexuality. Ostara is symbolized by the egg.

Otherworld

Another name for either the astral or unseen world, or for the Land of the Dead.

Pagan

Generic term for anyone who practices an earth or nature religion.

Pentagram

The ancient five-pointed star which has come to symbolize much of western Paganism. It is usually seen with its apex up, and can represent the four elements headed by the fifth element of spirit, or it can represent a human with her arms and legs spread to represent mind over matter. When encased in a circle, it is properly called a pentacle.

Power Hand

For purposes of magick, this is the hand which is dominant, usually the one with which you write.

Receptive Hand

For purposes of magick, this is the hand which is non-dominant, usually the one you do not use for writing.

Rede, Witches' Rede

This is the basic tenet of Pagan and Wiccan faiths: "As it harms none, do what you will." The Rede prohibits us from harming any other living thing and from violating anyone's free will.

Ritual

A systematic, formal, and prescribed set of actions and words whose purpose is to imprint a lasting change on the life and psyche of the participant.

Ritual Tools

Objects symbolizing a direction or an element in a ritual. These tools vary by Pagan tradition or with the tastes of the individual Witch. Each one usually represents one of the elements. Ritual tools may also be called magickal tools or elemental weapons in some traditions.

Sabbats

The eight solar festivals of the Witches' year. The word is derived from the Greek word *sabatu* meaning "to rest." The sabbats are Samhain (October 31), Winter Solstice or Yule, Imbolg (February 1 or 2), Spring Equinox or Ostra, Beltane (May 1), Summer Solstice or Litha, Lammas (August 1 or 2), and Autumn Equinox or Mabon.

Samhain

This sabbat is celebrated on the date now called Halloween, October 31. Samhain marked the beginning of winter for the Celts and was also their New Year's Day. It is a day to honor the crone aspect of the Goddess and the dying God who will be reborn at Yule. Samhain also marks the end of the harvest season.

Scrying

The divinatory act of gazing at an object until prophetic visions appear.

"So mote it be"

"Mote" is from an obsolete English word meaning "must." When uttered after an invocation, spell, etc., it seals the intent by voicing it as something that is now part of reality rather than an unformed wish.

Solitary

A Witch who works and worships alone without the aid of a larger coven. Some Witches are solitary by chance, meaning they would like to connect with others, and some are solitary by choice. The latter are usually older, more experienced Witches who find spiritual comfort in their solitude.

Spell

A specific magickal ritual designed for the purpose of obtaining, banishing, or changing one particular thing or condition.

Subconscious mind

That part of the mind that functions below the levels we are able to access in the course of a normal, waking day. This area stores symbolic knowledge, dreams, and the most minute details of every experience ever had by a person.

Summerland

A Wiccan term for the land of the dead.

Superconscious mind

The part of the mind that connects us with our higher selves and with the divine.

Sympathetic magick

A term coined by Sir James Frazer for a kind of magic based on the notion that like attracts like. The best example of sympathetic magick is the hunting dances of Native Americans. Hunters would dress as the animals they sought and enact the animals' slaying.

Sympathetic magick is the most common way spells are worked.

Tarot

A set of seventy-eight cards containing strong archetypal symbols that can be understood by the subconscious in order to do divination.

Threefold Law

The karmic principle of the Craft. It states that any energy released by an individual, either positive or negative, will return to its sender three times over.

Tradition

In Paganism, this refers to a specific branch of Paganism followed by any individual or coven. There are hundreds of these traditions, most drawn along ethnic or cultural lines, but several are modern amalgamations. The word "tradition" in this case is synonymous with "path."

Wand

A common ritual tool brought into the modern Craft through contact with ceremonial magicians. We also have evidence of their use by Celtic Druids. A wand can symbolize either the element of air and the direction of east or fire and south.

Wheel of Existence

The conceptualization of the spiraling movement of the universe. Sometimes this is conceived as a web. It unites all living things from all realms. What we put into this ever-turning wheel comes back to us threefold.

Wheel of the Year

A metaphor for the eternal cycle of time. The wheel of the year is symbolized by either a wreath, a ring, a snake holding its tail in its mouth, or an eight-spoked wheel.

Wicca

A tradition of Witchcraft with a huge following among neo-Pagans. *Wicca* is an Old English word meaning "to bend" or "to have wisdom." Though originally applied to only one English tradition of the Craft, today Wicca has become a term generally used to refer to many of the Pagan traditions from western and northern Europe, and has spawned many subtraditions.

Widdershins

The opposite of deosil, meaning to move backward. The word is from the Scottish tradition. Moving widdershins is the act of walking, working, or dancing counterclockwise in order to banish, diminish, or counter some force. Contrary to what many newcomers have been taught, moving widdershins is not necessarily a negative action but rather is a means for magick of decrease. Many Witches close their sacred circles by walking widdershins around them.

Witch

A name sometimes applied to Pagans of Celtic, Anglo, and/or Saxon Pagan traditions.

Yule

Yule is from an Old Norse word meaning wheel. It is another name for the sabbat that falls on the winter solstice. In some Scandinavian and Germanic Pagan traditions begin their spiritual new year on this date, thus the use of the term wheel to describe the changing of the year. Most of the Christmas customs observed today can be traced to Anglo-Saxon Pagan practices.

suggested reading

The list presented here represents only a small portion of books suitable for beginners or for those whose initiation is looming or has recently past. I chose these books only because I'm familiar with them, not because they are any better than others. As you take your first serious steps into Wicca, you should read everything you can get your hands on, and do so with a critical eye and an open mind. There is good and so-so to be found in any book, but even some very good ones may not be the right books for you. So please don't limit yourself to books on this list. Buy and study what inspires you and what seems to resonate with your unique talents and affinities.

books for beginners

Buckland, Raymond. *Buckland's Complete Book of Witchcraft*. St. Paul: Llewellyn Publications, 1987.

Crowley, Vivianne. *The Phoenix from the Flame*. Longmeade, UK: Aquarian, 1994.

Cunningham, Scott. *Wicca: A Guide for the Solitary Practitioner*. St. Paul: Llewellyn Publications, 1988.

Leek, Sybil. *The Complete Art of Witchcraft*. New York: Harper and Row, 1971.

RavenWolf, Silver. *Solitary Witch*. St. Paul: Llewellyn Publications, 2003.

———. *To Ride a Silver Broomstick*. St. Paul: Llewellyn Publications, 1993.

Starhawk. *The Spiral Dance*. San Francisco: Harper and Row, 1979.

general craft

Andrews, Ted. *Animal-Speak: The Spiritual and Magical Powers of Creatures Great and Small*. St. Paul: Llewellyn Publications, 1993.

Ashe, Geoffrey. *The Ancient Wisdom*. London: MacMillan, 1977.

Brennan, J. H. *Time Travel: A New Perspective*. St. Paul: Llewellyn Publications, 1997.

Cabot, Laurie. *The Power of the Witch*. New York: Delta Books, 1989.

Campanelli, Pauline and Dan. *Circles, Groves and Sanctuaries*. St. Paul: Llewellyn Publications, 1992.

————. *Ancient Ways*. St. Paul: Llewellyn Publications, 1991.

Cuchulain, Kerr. *The Wiccan Warrior*. St. Paul: Llewellyn Publications, 1997.

Denning, Melita, and Osborne Phillips. *Psychic Self-Defense and Well-Being*. St. Paul: Llewellyn Publications, 1980.

Farrar, Janet and Stewart. *The Witches' God*. Custer, WA: Phoenix Publishing, 1989.

————. *The Witches' Goddess*. Custer, WA: Phoenix Publishing, 1987.

Grimassi, Raven. *The Wiccan Mysteries*. St. Paul: Llewellyn Publications, 1997.

King, Serge. *Urban Shaman*. New York: Fireside Books, 1990.

Ludzia, Leo F. *The Space/Time Connection*. St. Paul: Llewellyn Publications, 1989.

MacLean, Adam. *The Triple Goddess*. Grand Rapids, MI: Phanes Press, 1989.

McCoy, Edain. *The Witch's Coven: Finding or Forming Your Own Circle*. Formerly *Inside a Witches' Coven*. St. Paul: Llewellyn Publications, 1997, 2003.

Matthews, Caitlin. *The Elements of the Goddess*. Longmeade, UK: Element Books, 1989.

Richardson, Alan. *Earth God Rising: The Return of the Male Mysteries*. St. Paul: Llewellyn Publications, 1992.

————. *Gate to the Moon: Mythical and Magical Doorways to the Otherworld*. Wellingborough, UK: Aquarian Press, 1984.

Roderick, Timothy. *Dark Moon Mysteries*. St. Paul: Llewellyn Publications, 1992.

Rosenfeld, Albert, ed. *Mind and Supermind*. New York: Holt, Rinehart and Winston, 1977.

Sabrina, Lady. *Reclaiming the Power*. St. Paul: Llewellyn Publications, 1992.

Savage, Candace. *Witch: The Wild Ride from Wicked to Wicca*. Vancouver, BC: Grey Stone Books, 2000.

Spencer, John and Anne. *The Encyclopedia of Ghosts and Spirits*. London: Headline Books, 1992.

Stewart, R. J. *The Underworld Initiation: A Journey Towards Psychic Transformation*. Wellingborough, UK: Aquarian, 1985.

Telesco, Patricia. *A Kitchen Witch's Cookbook*. St. Paul: Llewellyn Publications, 1994.

———. *Urban Pagan: Magickal Living in a 9–5 World*. St. Paul: Llewellyn Publications, 1993.

Valiente, Doreen. *The Rebirth of Witchcraft*. Custer, WA: Phoenix Publishing Inc., 1989.

herbs and gemstones

Cunningham, Scott. *Cunningham's Encyclopedia of Crystal, Gem and Metal Magic*. St. Paul: Llewellyn Publications, 1988.

———. *Cunningham's Encyclopedia of Magical Herbs*. St. Paul: Llewellyn Publications, 1985.

history

Davidson, H. R. Ellis. *The Lost Beliefs of Northern Europe*. London: Routledge and Kegan Paul, 1993.

Hutton, Ronald. *The Pagan Religions of the Ancient British Isles*. Oxford: Blackwell Press, 1991.

———. *The Stations of the Sun: A History of the Ritual Year in Britain*. Oxford, England: Oxford University Press, 1996.

Loomis, Roger Sherman. *The Grail: From Celtic Myth to Christian Symbol*. Princeton, NJ: Princeton University Press, 1991.

Rogo, Scott. *Parapsychology: A Century of Inquiry*. New York: Taplinger, 1975.

Williams, Selma R., and Pamela J. Williams Adelman. *Riding the Nightmare: Women and Witchcraft from the Old World to Colonial Salem*. 1978. Reprint, New York: HarperPerenial, 1992.

Wilson, David. *Anglo-Saxon Paganism*. London: Routledge, 1992.

magick and spellcraft

Ashcroft-Nowicki, Dolores and J. H. Brennan. *The Magical Use of Thoughtforms*. St. Paul: Llewellyn Publications, 2001.

Bonewitz, Isaac. *Real Magic*. York Beach, ME: Samuel-Weiser, 1989.

Buckland, Raymond. *Practical Color Magic*. St. Paul: Llewellyn Publications, 1986.

González-Wippler, Migene. *The Complete Book of Spells, Ceremonies and Magic*. St. Paul: Llewellyn Publications, 1988.

Green, Marian. *Elements of Natural Magic*. Longmeade, UK: Element Books, 1989.

Grimassi, Raven. *Wiccan Magick*. St. Paul: Llewellyn Publications, 1998.

McCoy, Edain. *Making Magick*. St. Paul: Llewellyn Publications, 1997.

Malbrough, Ray T. *Charms, Spells and Formulas*. St. Paul: Llewellyn Publications, 1989.

Sheba, Lady. *The Grimoire of Lady Sheba*. St. Paul: Llewellyn Publications, 1971.

Thorsson, Edred. *Futhark: A Handbook of Rune Magick*. York Beach, ME: Samuel Weiser, 1984.

Valiente, Doreen. *Natural Magic*. Custer, WA: Phoenix, 1980.

Weinstein, Marion. *Positive Magic*. Custer, WA: Phoenix, 1980.

meditation and visualization

Clement, Stephanie. *Meditation for Beginners: Techniques for Awareness, Mindfullness & Relaxation*. St. Paul: Llewellyn Publications, 2003.

Galehorn, Yasmine. *Trancing the Witch's Wheel*. St. Paul: Llewellyn Publications, 1997.

Gardner Adelaide. *Meditation: A Practical Study*. Wheaton, IL: Quest Books, 1968.

Gawain, Shakti. *Creative Visualization*. 1955. Reprint, Berkeley: Whatever Publishing, 1975.

Judith, Anodea. *Wheels of Life: A User's Guide to the Chakra System*. St. Paul: Llewellyn Publications, 1986.

Sutphen, Dick. *Finding Your Answers Within*. New York: Pocket Books, 1989.

mythology

Ashe, Geoffrey. *Mythology of the British Isles*. North Pomfret, VT: Trafalgar Square Publishers, 1990.

Campbell, Joseph. *The Hero with a Thousand Faces*. Princeton, NJ: Princeton University Press, 1973.

Davidson, H. R. Ellis. *Myths and Symbols in Pagan Europe*. Syracuse, NY: The University of Syracuse Press, 1988.

Gundarsson, Kveldulf. *Teutonic Religion*. St. Paul: Llewellyn Publications, 1993.

VonFranz, Marie-Louise. *Creation Myths*. Boston: Shambhala Publications, 1972.

ritual

Adler, Margot. *Drawing Down the Moon*. (Rev. ed.). Boston: Beacon Press, 1986.

Campanelli, Pauline and Dan. *Pagan Rites of Passage*. St. Paul: Llewellyn, 1994, 2000.

Farrar, Janet and Stewart. *Eight Sabbats for Witches*. Custer, WA: Phoenix Publishing, 1981.

McCoy, Edain. *Magick and Rituals of the Moon*. St. Paul: Llewellyn Publications, 1994.

———. *The Sabbats*. St. Paul: Llewellyn Publications, 1994.

Rhea, Maeve, and Barbara E. Vordenbrueggen. *Summoning Forth the Wiccan Gods and Goddesses: The Magick of Invocation and Evocation*. New York: Citadel Press, 1999.

sabbats

RavenWolf, Silver. *Halloween: Customs, Recipes & Spells*. St. Paul: Llewellyn Publications, 1999.

Morrison, Dorothy. *Yule: A Celebration of Light and Warmth*. St. Paul: Llewellyn Publications, 2000.

K, Amber, and Azrael Arynn. *Candlemas: Feast of Flames*. St. Paul: Llewellyn Publications, 2001.

McCoy, Edain. *Ostara: Customs, Spells & Rituals for the Rites of Spring*. St. Paul: Llewellyn Publications, 2002.

Grimassi, Raven. *Beltane: Springtime Rituals, Lore & Celebration*. St. Paul: Llewellyn Publications, 2001

Franklin, Anna. *Midsummer: Magical Celebrations of the Summer Solstice*. St. Paul: Llewellyn Publications, 2002.

Franklin, Anna, and Paul Mason. *Lammas: Celebrating the Fruits of the First Harvest*. St. Paul: Llewellyn Publications, 2001.

Madden, Kristin. *Mabon: Celebrating the Autumn Equinox*. St. Paul: Llewellyn Publications, 2002.

index

Free Magazine

Read unique articles by Llewellyn authors, recommendations by experts, and information on new releases. To receive a **free** copy of Llewellyn's consumer magazine, *New Worlds of Mind & Spirit,* simply call 1-877-NEW-WRLD or visit our website at www.llewellyn.com and click on *New Worlds.*

☾ LLEWELLYN ORDERING INFORMATION

Order Online:
Visit our website at www.llewellyn.com, select your books, and order them on our secure server.

Order by Phone:
- Call toll-free within the U.S. at 1-877-NEW-WRLD (1-877-639-9753). Call toll-free within Canada at 1-866-NEW-WRLD (1-866-639-9753)
- We accept VISA, MasterCard, and American Express

Order by Mail:
Send the full price of your order (MN residents add 7% sales tax) in U.S. funds, plus postage & handling to:
Llewellyn Worldwide
P.O. Box 64383, Dept. 0-7387-0514-4
St. Paul, MN 55164-0383, U.S.A.

Postage & Handling:
Standard (U.S., Mexico, & Canada). If your order is:
Up to $25.00, add $3.50
$25.01 - $48.99, add $4.00
$49.00 and over, FREE STANDARD SHIPPING
(Continental U.S. orders ship UPS. AK, HI, PR, & P.O. Boxes ship USPS 1st class. Mex. & Can. ship PMB.)

International Orders:
Surface Mail: For orders of $20.00 or less, add $5 plus $1 per item ordered. For orders of $20.01 and over, add $6 plus $1 per item ordered.

Air Mail:
Books: Postage & Handling is equal to the total retail price of all books in the order.
Non-book items: Add $5 for each item.

Orders are processed within 2 business days.
Please allow for normal shipping time. Postage and handling rates subject to change.